STEADFAST
LEADERSHIP

50 Tips to Make Your Best *BETTER*

BRETT M. DAVENPORT

2-Time International #1 Best-Selling Author of
"Leadership Playbook" & "Coaching Your Way to Success"

Published by Empire Financial Network, Inc.

Copyright © 2024 Brett M. Davenport

All rights reserved. No part of this book may be reproduced or transmitted in any form or by any means, electronic or mechanical, including photocopying, recording or by any information storage and retrieval system without written permission of the publisher, except for the inclusion of brief quotations in a review.

Printed in the United States of America

Davenport, Brett M.

    Steadfast Leadership: 50 Tips to Make Your Best Better / by Brett M. Davenport

Library of Congress Cataloging-in-Publication Data

ISBN: Hardcover: 978-0-578-32794-5

           Paperback: 979-8-218-18496-4

Cover/Interior Design by: Teagarden Designs
dawn@teagardendesigns.com

Warning—Disclaimer

The purpose of this book is to educate and entertain. The author or publisher does not guarantee that anyone following the techniques, suggestions, tips, ideas, or strategies will become successful. The author and publisher shall have neither liability nor responsibility to anyone with respect to any loss or damage caused, or alleged to be caused, directly or indirectly by the information contained in this book.

DEDICATION

This is a shout out to all of us who are currently going through a challenge that when we look up it appears to be such a monumental climb that we allow doubt to control us...

Fact: Over my short lifetime, personally as well as professionally; that is 59 short years, I've yet to meet someone who hasn't been blessed with the opportunity to experience "monumental" challenge in their life, but those who embrace these opportunities and convert them to strengths become gifted beyond their potential!

I hope this book provides a different lens in regards to challenges, so that we welcome the next one for the purpose it provides ... *LET's GO!*

WIN!

#1

Acknowledgments

Today, I would like to recognize the "CHAMPIONS" that I'm blessed to Coach every day!

Your relentless pursuit to improve your very best, while creating a CULTURE of LIFE/WORK BALANCE is the #1 reason, of many, for your continued SUCCESS within your industry and beyond!

Your unique sustainability & unwavering PURPOSE for PEOPLE and FAMILY is admirable and rare as an Executive Business Leader/Owner!

The unselfish approach you commit to your TEAM's CAREER DEVELOPMENT is 2nd to none and a huge competitive advantage!

Finally, THANK YOU for always being 1st in line when it comes to ACCOUNTABILITY & always embracing an Expect to Win Mindset! I feel privileged to be on YOUR TEAM!

You Rock! Coach

I would also like to recognize the ONE Person who inspires me every day to be my very best and the uplifting desire to challenge that… my Beautiful Bride Joanne of 32 years!

Since my last book, Joanne is a Breast Cancer Survivor and her POSITIVE MINDSET to attack this awful disease is without a doubt the best example of "Expect to Win" I've witnessed in my lifetime!

Thank you, Sweetheart, for ALL YOU DO and LEADING our FAMILY with laser focused Goal Attainment!

I LOVE YOU!

In the spirit of acknowledgment, I'm so PROUD of our 2 Boys, Harrison and Connor, for an abundant of characteristics, but the ONE that stands tall is their "Lead by Example Attitude!"

THANK YOU, Men, for your Generous Heart, Steadfast Leadership, Determination to Grow and Tenacious COMMITMENT to FAMILY!

Your #1 Fan, Love Ya! Dad

Finally, I'd like to acknowledge our Son, Connor's Lovely Bride and our Wonderful Daughter-in-Law, Allie!

Allie, you bring Sunshine every day with that Warm Smile, your Glowing Personality, Passion for FAMILY and your POSITIVE ATTITUDE!

We look forward to many more decades of FUN TOGETHER!!

We Love You! Dad

What Others are Saying About Brett M. Davenport...

"Many coaches in our industry are limited by the concepts and knowledge they share, based on their prior experience, and fail to evolve with the industry as it is forever changing. Having worked with "Coach Davenport" for the past 12 years, his insights, strategies, and motivational support allows me to narrow my focus and execute on the highest priorities to ensure the greatest impact with my team! Coach is always focused on continuous improvement through what he calls "Areas of Development"! Some examples of those insights and strategies include; Recruiting #1 draft picks, one-of-a-kind goal setting process, running productive campaigns, accountability on purpose, 100% execution type mindset and creating a successful strategic vision for the future!"

Robert Milliman, CMFC®, Senior Vice President
National Sales Manager-IBD
Head of Practice Management
First Eagle Investments

"I have worked with Brett as my personal coach for the last 12 years. He has been critical in helping take my ideas from vision to reality and has brought structure and accountability to my goals. "Coach" can be a difference maker in driving success both professionally and personally!"

Jeff Duckworth, CRPC, Head of Intermediary Distribution

"Coach Brett helped me to dig deep and tap into my past to solve my present—unlocking a winning formula to unite sales, service, and operation teams for 34 distinctly different cultures to ONE resulting in a category of one provider. What is the moment, situation, or obstacle that you worked through that most closely resembles where you are today? The moment when what winning looks like and feels like was engraved on your soul, driving you to exceeding outcomes and success beyond your imagination; if you tap into it, it never ends."

Kasey Robertson Price, Leader in the TPA market, former entrepreneur and founding owner of Retirement Strategies Inc.

"Brett has a unique, proven approach to developing leaders and highly effective teams. His approach is intuitive and very effective. Whether you lead a team, or are just trying to become the best version of you, Coach can help!"

Gary Tankersley, Head of Sales & Distribution

"It takes a lot to be really good in your career and in life. But how do the good become great? Brett is "Coach" to many of the best and when you experience working with him then you know why. Coach is instrumental in working with me and my partners to channel our vision, passion, and focus towards being great. Our company would not be as successful and on its way to greatness if it was not for our working with Coach Brett. Thanks Coach, we are grateful!"

Jeffrey Segal, CEO and Founder
C.I.G. Private Wealth Management

"Brett has been my executive coach for many years. He's one of the only people that I can say holds me accountable and pushes me to be my best. His strategy and tactics for goal setting, and ultimately achieving, lead to success after success. He coached me through some difficult situations, and always guides me and helps to see me through to the other side. I would highly recommend him to anyone looking to go after whatever you want in life. Both personally and professionally."

Stephanie Noris, Founder, NorBella Inc

"Coach Brett has written a practical, powerful book that will help anyone in a leadership role become disciplined. I have the pleasure of working closely with him. He is exceptional at influencing human behavior to help achieve extraordinary results."

Aaron McIsaac, Sales Leader

"Coach Davenport delivers! He has been my professional and personal coach for nearly 6 years. In every meeting, he brings a high level of energy and keeps me focused on what really matters. His coaching methods allow you to see past the "noise" and to prioritize your time to focus on the goals that are most important to drive your business forward and make your personal life more fulfilling. He is professional and highly motivational. If you are going to make an investment in yourself, I encourage you to consider Coach Davenport!"

Abigail Benham, Head of National Accounts

"Brett Davenport = COACH + PASSION + CARING + GRIT + ACCOUNTABILITY

Coach—someone whose job is to teach people to improve at a sport, skill, or school subject

Passion—intense, driving, or overmastering feeling or conviction

Caring—feeling or showing concern for or kindness to others

Grit—courage and resolve; strength of character

Accountability—Expect it, Embrace it and Own it

This is the secret sauce that Brett brings to the table or put another way, if you are wise enough to be 100% committed to Brett's approach and teachings... You Will Experience... Brett + You = Success!!"

Ross W. Kraft, LUTCF, GBDS, CWCA
Vice President Strategic Business Advisor

"I had the pleasure of working with Coach Brett for all of 2022. He has been by far the most impactful business coach I have ever had, and I hope to continue to work with him in the future. He has done a great job helping me reflect on my leadership journey so far and has provided guidance and expertise on how I can grow as a leader in the future. Many of the coaching tips that he has shared with me I keep top of mind every day!"

Jeff Tallia, Internal Sales Director

"Brett Davenport has been my best friend, my partner and my husband for the past 32 years! He is the most honest, hardworking, positive person I have ever met. He is dedicated day in and day out to his Coaching Members in order to help them achieve their goals. He treats all of his Coaching Members with the respect they deserve and shows them levels of success they did not even know were possible.

Brett is ALWAYS a "Present" Father and Husband making time for Family 1st, with a healthy life/work balance! One characteristic that has impressed me over our lifetime together…is that he practices what he coaches 100% of the time!

I love you so much Brett and I look forward to many more decades with you and our growing family!

Congratulations on another AWESOME Book!"

Joanne L. Davenport, MBA, Accounting Specialist, HR One

"Persistent, patient, effective are words that come to mind when I think of Brett. I got to know "Coach" when he volunteered to join a fundraising team for Expect Miracles Foundation's Distance Challenge to raise funds for our cancer research and financial assistance programs. From the moment he committed to the fundraiser, Coach brought strategy, passion, energy, and teamwork to bear in helping his team become the top fundraising team. Getting the job done and having fun doing it—I really enjoy working with Coach!"

Frank Heavey, Executive Director at Expect Miracles Foundation—Financial Services Against Cancer

"A conversation with Coach D is guaranteed to spark massive change in your life. Regardless of whom you are where you're at in life or what your vision is—he will guide and challenge you towards becoming the best version of you! He is known for working with high level leaders, yet, he won't shy away from investing into young and aspiring leaders and entrepreneurs. Coach D has devoted a generous amount of time and energy into my development as 22 year old... I ask Coach what I can do to do give back to him—his answer is simple... "The one thing you can do for me is to become a wildly successful entrepreneur who has great leadership skills, because that's what this world needs most. Thanks to Coach D's help... I know I am on my way there!"

Jack Ryan, Director of Business Development

"Brett Davenport is an amazing "coach". It's not just his knowledge and experience that brings a team together. He has an amazing way of taking people from OK, good and even excellent and driving them up to be what not even they thought they could do. Always positive and encouraging, anyone would be fortunate to have him as a coach."

Kathleen Mee, Independent Education
Management Professional

"I have had the opportunity to work with Coach over the last 5 years. His passion and drive are infectious and he challenges you to bring your best! It's an honor and privilege to work with him!"

Laurie Bricker, Senior National Account Manager,
Vice President Nationwide

Door Number 1
"I have had the honor and privilege of knowing and being associated with Brett for over 25 years. Let me share some observations about this man. Brett has known for many years what was needed to get him where he wanted to go and what was necessary to get him there. I was always amazed at his determination, dedication to family, community, and work, and his ability to come from behind and finish first. Brett is a motivated motivator!"

Door Number 2
"Coach Davenport is a master at wearing different hats. The commonality he brings to these different roles is his enthusiasm, analytical ability, and attitude. Whether it is a sports team, educational pursuit, writing books, business ventures, family, community, or charity....Coach is there 110 percent! It has been fulfilling for me to watch his continuing journey."

Door number 3
"If you or your organization needs a "tune up," it would be my recommendation to call Brett "Coach" Davenport. He knows all about mediocrity, and how to propel it to magnificent. Peruse his resume, read his books, and study his company. A call to this man may change you and/or your organization for the better and to strive for the best. Coach would probably say, it is a lot about "attitude, expectation and ACCOUNTABILITY!"

Raymond Quick, President at
Quick Development Company

"I have known Brett for over 30 years and has always been my biggest supporter. Brett cares deeply for his family and friends. He has helped me and many clients find work life balance so they do not miss out on the moments in life that actually matter."

Terri Gleason, Area Manager, Wegmans

"Leadership: Merriam-Webster defines it as; an act or instance of leading. I however, expand their definitions to include; one's ability to consistently lead others to perform beyond their expectations. Coach Davenport exemplifies my definition of Leadership... as a Husband, Father, Colleague, Friend and Coach! Brett "Coach" Davenport has successfully led individuals, organizations and teams to heights otherwise not achievable! It's been my experience that Brett's formula of applying concepts of positive thinking, determination, accountability, goal setting and commitment to "TEAM" are the foundation of his results-based success!

It is my privilege to be his Brother, Friend and Student!"

Brent Davenport, Managing Principal, Infrastructure Design, Inc.

"Brett is a gifted student and teacher of leadership who inspires the best in others."

Mary Quist-Newins, MBA, MSFS, CFP®, CLU®, ChFC®
CEO and President, Moneyweave® Academy, Inc.

"Brett has been my professional life coach for 6 years now—he is wonderful to work with! He has exceptional expertise in leadership, coaching and motivation. He has challenged me to hold myself accountable each and every day in both my professional and personal life. He has changed my thought process and behavior in ways I never would have thought. After each session with Brett, I leave feeling energetic, motivated and empowered as a leader, wife and mother.

I highly endorse Coach Brett! #1 TEAM!"

Leah Ramondt, National Sales Director

"Brett Davenport has been my business and personal coach for the past 5 years. He is personally invested in helping me to achieve success in both areas. Brett has helped me to continually take a step back and focus on the most critical areas of responsibility for me and for my firm. His guidance has been professionally and personally rewarding. Thank you Coach!"

Ann Smith, Retired Chief Operating Officer and Chief Compliance Officer at Heritage Financial Services

"Brett (Coach) Davenport is the most positive person I know! He is insightful and motivating. His extensive knowledge and experience allow him to help you look at achieving both professional and personal goals from a new perspective. He challenges you to be the best you can be. Working with Coach you realize he is fully invested and sincerely wants you to achieve your goals, "major in the majors", be #1."

Holly S. Manning, Managing Director at InspereX

"I have known Brett "Coach" Davenport on both a personal and professional level for over 25 years. The strategies and principles discussed in Brett's books are transformative. Brett lives his life every day by these principles. The smile you see on his face is genuine and never leaves. He is the most positive and upbeat person I have ever met. As a young professional Brett mentored me. His guidance and encouragement changed my life. The same guidance he gave me is now written in the pages of his books. These principles and strategies changed my life and help me achieve career goals that I never thought were attainable. They will have the same effect on the readers of his books. Brett is an amazing man. His books are amazing too. I'm proud to call him my friend, mentor and Coach ... reading his books you can too!!"

Tom Clark III, Owner Operator at McDonald's Corporation

"Genuine and outrageously positive are the words that come to mind when I think of Brett. I've been working with Brett for 4 years now and I always look forward to our next call. He helps me understand on a deeper level what's really important in my life both professionally and personally, he inspires me to be the best I can be and keeps me focused on the next steps necessary to achieve my goals. He is a great motivator and an excellent communicator with sound advice. The world is a better place with Brett, thanks for being you and all that you do!"

Janet Barrett, ChFC®, CDFA® Wealth Advisor at Carson Wealth

Contents

Acknowledgments 5
Tip #1: Use Purpose to Win the Race 19
Tip #2: Know Your Team like the Back of Your Hand 23
Tip #3: Develop New Producers 27
Tip #4: Start a Leadership Journey Journal Habit 31
Tip #5: Publish Newsletters to Acknowledge Go-Getters . 35
Tip #6: Learn to Earn 43
Tip #7: Conduct 1:11 Minute Coaching Sessions 47
Tip #8: Avoid the 4 **P**-ers 51
Tip #9: Perform a 52-Week Look-Back 55
Tip #10: Practice R^3 for Maximum Performance 59
Tip #11: Tear Down Silos, Build Bridges 67
Tip #12: Eliminate the *Perfect* Enemy 71
Tip #13: Call the Play 75
Tip #14: Concentrate on Cadence 79
Tip #15: Execute the Plan 83
Tip #16: Be a Thermostat 93
Tip #17: Know Your Brand's Position 97
Tip #18: Win with Flawless Follow-Up 101
Tip #19: Empower Your Executive Assistant 105
Tip #20: Ride Tailwinds, Respect Headwinds 109
Tip #21: Produce a Study Map to Pass 113
Tip #22: Act Aggressively, with Patience 117
Tip #23: Name One Word for the Coming Year 121
Tip #24: Apply the 24-Hour Rule 125

Tip #25: Experience Role play, with Rules	129
Tip #26: Consciously Choose Leadership	133
Tip #27: Earn Respect with L.E.A.D.E.R.S.	137
Tip #28: Recite the Champion's Creed	141
Tip #29: Listen and Be Memorable	145
Tip #30: Plant Seeds	151
Tip #31: Respond to Your "C2A"	159
Tip #32: Maintain Your Message	163
Tip #33: Raise Three Process Pillars	167
Tip #34: Build Your Practice the Referral Way	171
Tip #35: Put Me in COACH	181
Tip #36: Coach the Coaches	185
Tip #37: Communicate with Purpose	189
Tip #38: Prepare for Launch	193
Tip #39: Slow Down to Speed Up	203
Tip #40: Replace Stubborn with S.M.A.R.T.	207
Tip #41: Know You're Only One YES Away	217
Tip #42: Negotiate to E.A.R.N.	221
Tip #43: Seize Accountability, Delegate Responsibility	225
Tip #44: Prescribe Your Own P.I.P.	229
Tip #45: Cause an Effect	239
Tip #46: Keep it Clean	243
Tip #47: Take the Most Important Step	247
Tip #48: Finish It	251
Tip #49: Treat all Days Equally	259
Tip #50: Go from Worst to First	263
This Doesn't Have to be Goodbye	275
About Brett M. Davenport	279

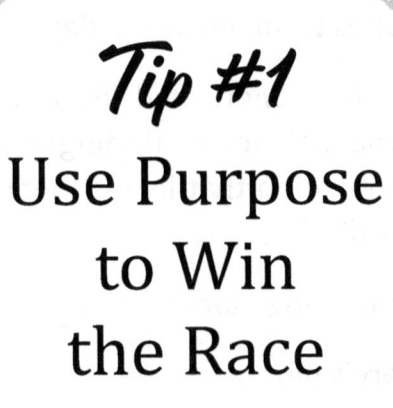

Tip #1
Use Purpose to Win the Race

Motivation is helpful, but purpose is the only reason you'll need it.

When you open your eyes in the morning and struggle with the notion of getting out of bed, your first thought might be *I need motivation*. That motivation—whether it's coffee, human interaction, or the need to earn a paycheck—will work. It worked today, in fact.

But tomorrow, you will once again be searching for a reason to drag yourself out into the world, only to find yourself seeking new pieces of motivation so you can reach milestones throughout the day.

What makes highly motivated leaders successful? Do they move through their days finding inspiration around them? The motivation that keeps them energized and moving forward?

Or is there something more?

Of course, there's more.

Conscious leaders aren't trudging blindly through each day, hoping they'll find the motivation they need. Instead, their eyes snap open when the alarm rings, they hop out of bed, and they go about their day with an overwhelming sense of desire that comes from living out their passion.

That's because they aren't just motivated. They have a PURPOSE.

How to Define and Find Your Purpose

You've heard the story of the tortoise and the hare, right? The hare sprinted ahead with agility and speed, but soon became distracted. He was motivated, for sure. But that motivation was short-lived, with no passion or staying power.

The tortoise, on the other hand, acted purposefully. He moved slowly, but steadily...all the while focusing on the finish line.

We all know which character won, and it's a great illustration of Motivation vs. Purpose.

When you have a purpose, and you're living it every day, you'll never have to wonder if you're on the right path. You'll never dread going to work or practice. You will never, ever lack the motivation to be the best you can be or to inspire others to do the same.

Many leaders-to-be haven't yet found their purpose. Or, they believe their purpose is something shallow, like earning lots of money or gaining notoriety. These types of things offer short-lived satisfaction. And you guessed it: when the thrill wears off, there's a need for new motivation.

Purpose, on the other hand, doesn't grow stale. It's the thing you know you were born to achieve, and so dedicating your life to making it happen is not only bearable—it inspires pure joy, every day!

If you haven't yet discovered your purpose, it can help to ask some questions:

- What bothers you? What pain would you like to relieve? What problem would you like to fix?
- What's the one thing you would do every day, even if you weren't getting paid?
- What do your friends know and love about you?
- Where do your natural talents lie?
- What types of compliments mean the most to you?

- In what types of situations does your intuition speak the loudest?
- When you help other people, what types of reactions make you feel most fulfilled?
- Think back on your life so far. In what instances did you feel the most rewarded, content, or accomplished?
- Where do you see yourself in ten years? Twenty? Thirty? What will you be most proud of, and what fond memories will you have?
- What difference do you want to make in the world? In your community? In your company? In your organization? In your team? In your family? In your life? Or in your... *anything*, because you are 100% in control.

When you have a purpose that allows you to express your passion, and to produce an outcome that inspires genuine pride, then you're living your Purpose.

Motivation might help to get you through to lunch, but Purpose will drive you to the end of your career and beyond.

"Motivation comes and goes, but PURPOSE that is anchored in your mind, heart & soul lasts a lifetime!"

—Coach Davenport

Tip #2
Know Your Team like the Back of Your Hand

Discover your team, uncover victory.

You are familiar with the back of your hand, or so the idiom goes. And you should know your team at least that well.

Leaders can have the tendency to believe that just because a team is accomplishing something related to business, politics, sports...then there's no need to know each member of that team on a personal level. In fact, I know many leaders who believe that would be an invasion of privacy or the crossing of some sort of boundary.

On the contrary, we are REAL people making up squads, crews, businesses...teams of all sorts. These teams are not machines. They're not comprised of automaton units. They are groups of living, breathing human beings who are not only unique individuals, but individuals with genuine needs.

First and foremost, we have an innate human need to connect to other humans. Only after that happens can all the facets of proficient and effective teamwork be set into motion.

As a team leader, it is your responsibility to facilitate that condition.

Know This About Your Team...

People rarely quit their jobs. More often, they quit their bosses. As a leader, it's crucial that you build a strong bond with your team members, and that starts with showing interest not only in what they do, but in who they are.

Initiating interactions that result in personal discovery is a foundational element of relationship-building. And when you retain the information you've learned about your team members and refer back to it...that builds and reinforces trust.

Gather this information in a natural, conversational way, committing it to memory:

- **Names**: This might seem like a no-brainer, but remembering the names of your direct reports is essential, and the importance of recalling those names is often dismissed with statements like, "I'm terrible with names." Be the one who's different. Be the one who remembers their name, and they'll remember how that made them feel.

- **Names of their Spouses and Children**: For many of your team members, their families are of the utmost importance. Take an interest in what they're proud of. Take note of the names and upcoming events they share. Then ask about those people (by name) and how things are going.

- **Birthdays and Anniversaries**: Nothing builds relationships like making what's important to them important to you, too. Acknowledge those dates. Celebrate!

- **Hobbies and Interests**: What do your direct reports do on the weekends? Ask questions so you can discover more about them through their hobbies, or find interests you have in common and share experiences.

Remember what human nature dictates: Everyone wants others to take an interest in them—even the most introverted. When leaders show interest in what their direct reports care about, those team members feel vital, important...like they matter. Close working relationships will result, and brand loyalty will blossom.

Take the time to learn about your team members. It seems like such a simple thing, and yet, it demonstrates so much. Take an interest in them, and they will show a vested interest in the team as a whole.

Know them like the back of your hand...and you'll have all hands on deck.

"If we are always looking for something new, we will never get to experience the value of something old."

—*Coach Davenport*

Tip #3
Develop New Producers

The Fledgling Formula relies as heavily on independence as it does on support.

When we think of a "New Producer" entering the sales team, we often focus on the *Producer*, when in fact, intrinsic value also lies in the *New*. With that newness comes the opportunity to cultivate an affinity for the brand's culture, loyalty to the brand's vision, and a *desire* to *produce*.

Many Sales Leaders shy away from newness, in favor of experience.

Experience comes with preconceptions and long-held beliefs that may not be in alignment with the Sales Leader's goals. And so, the most success-obsessed sales leaders seek out new talent, knowing that with the right formula, they can surpass even the most grandiose expectations.

How?

They acquire that New Producer, raise them upright, guide them toward autonomy, and then kick them off the nest's edge so they can SOAR.

Responsibility isn't a drag. Broken down, it is the ABILITY to RESPOND. When new talent is taught to embrace that, the first year (or the first lap, as we call it) will exceed expectations.

From Development to Delivery: The Fledgling Formula

New talent is just that: a raw, untapped, underutilized ability that has the *potential* to produce. Left unleashed, willy-nilly, that raw talent has the same production capability as a featherless hatch-ling that's been forced to try to fly. Both will fall flat.

A baby bird has unlimited potential to soar. However, he/she hasn't yet acquired the tools to make that happen.

That's where the Sales Leader comes in.

Raw talent is contained within unique individuals who possess varying concentrations and levels of aptitude. And so, it would make sense that in order to extract potential, we need a structured, proven system for not only growing those feathers, but providing guidance as we impart the knowledge necessary for flight.

In just one year, (52 short weeks) New Talent can become a New Producer, soaring alongside your most accomplished salespeople.

Here's how:

- **1st 90 Days**: The Sales Leader is responsible, for going about business as usual. The New Talent observes, asks questions, and absorbs. The Sales Leader owns successes and failures.

- **2nd 90 Days**: The Sales Leader *and* The New Talent (soon to be The New Producer) are equally responsible for results, working together with open communication and unlimited question-asking and answering.

- **3rd 90 Days**: The New Producer is wholly responsible for executing what he or she has been taught, and is expected to grow equally from responses like "No," "Not Now," and "Yes" as they forge forward toward Goal Attainment. Their acquisition of leads (mainly from COI and referrals), along with tenuous follow-up and accountable activity, will accelerate their efficiency of flight. The Sales Leader / Coach will never be far away—always available for consultation—as communication of results in areas that matter continues on a consistent basis.

- **4th 90 Days**: The Sales Leader cuts the New Producer loose! There will be final prep for flight, words of encouragement, and yes… the proverbial push from the nest.

By the end of the first lap around, your New Producer will have had a successful foundational year, with all the skills necessary for soaring independently, beneficial not only to him or herself, but the entire business.

When the first year exceeds expectations, a precedent is set. The New Producer is now viewed as an invaluable asset—a star—and that's the best kind of incentive to keep on soaring!

"A culture of leadership is when your team feels your presence when you aren't present."

—Coach Davenport

Tip #4
Start a Leadership Journey Journal Habit

What we write becomes real.

When we hear the word *Habit*, there's a tendency to assign a negative connotation. We know about alcohol habits, drug habits, smoking habits, gambling habits, poor eating habits…and it becomes easy to believe that habits are destructive elements.

And yet, healthy, constructive habits can be just as addictive as those vices.

Effective leaders have been talking about the addictive benefits of journaling for decades, and yet the "J word" still elicits an eye roll that can be felt around the world.

Why? Is it because people don't enjoy writing? Or because they feel they don't have time? Or because they're uncomfortable with self-discovery?

The real reason is that they haven't yet begun to understand the impact it can have on their leadership roles, or on the leadership roles of those who will follow.

Your Leadership Journey Journal

There's a short story about two leaders:

> *One went about his day, changing attitudes and lives, never writing anything down. When he died, his methods and legacy went with him. His mistakes would be repeated. His victories would go unrecognized—claimed by others, or never duplicated.*

> *The other journaled daily, writing about his missteps as well as his discoveries. He referred back to that journal often, reminding himself of what was possible and remembering which trails led nowhere. When he was gone, his name was not forgotten. Those who continued his legacy simply couldn't forget what he had shared with them.*

You are a prolific leader—or at least you plan to be. You want to leave a legacy of importance for generations to come. You want your grandchildren to hear stories about the difference you made in the world, and you want future leaders in your organization to use your wisdom to usher the company or team into the future.

Maybe you never thought about it that way, but let's be honest: You want all that, right?

Learning to be an effective leader is a voyage filled with potholes, pitfalls, peaks, and rainbow-painted horizons. It's a lifetime's worth of work. And yet, there's a tendency to focus on the results, or the accomplishments achieved by the end of one's career—when the real story is contained within the journey.

How will that journey be chronicled? How will it be shared? And how can both you and future generations learn from it?

Keeping a Leadership Journey Journal is the answer.

Here are a few ways you can use it to enhance your leadership, the legacy of that leadership, and the leadership of those who follow:

Journaling…

- compels us to reflect on what's working and what's not
- improves communication
- encourages daily mindfulness, as we think about writing down what has happened
- increases focus on goals through reflection
- enhances empathy and emotional intelligence, for relationship nurturing
- improves memory, because what we write becomes real and more easily recalled

- intensifies self-discipline by creating a productive habit
- aids in acceptance and healing of distressing situations
- bolsters self-confidence with a sense of "I can do this"
- develops creativity
- creates a chronological history of your leadership journey, for you and future generations
- Every leader who breaks into uncharted territory is a pioneer. And the territory he or she covers paves the way for future leaders to be even more conscious and courageous.

If that journey is not chronicled through journaling, then territory that has been navigated will persist as "uncharted," leaving the ground you've covered unrecognized.

Don't let your life's work go unrecorded.

Tell your story, for the sake of your leadership journey and its legacy.

> *"TODAY is Non-Refundable, Capture it!"*
>
> *—Coach Davenport*

Tip #5
Publish Newsletters to Acknowledge Go-Getters

What we publicly appreciate is personally magnified.

Leaders have a responsibility to build relationships on an individual basis—between themselves and every direct report. They are responsible for offering feedback and guidance; praise and recognition.

However, accolades cannot bloom to their highest potential within a vacuum. Encouragement and compliments confined to cubicles and delivered behind closed doors have limited effectiveness—whereas public praise has a way of compounding all the good things we expect.

We often think of a newsletter as a way to update customers and markets about what's new, and what benefits they can expect. However, we shouldn't forget that newsletters offer a tremendous platform for publicly acknowledging those players within our teams who are exceeding expectations.

Not only do team members up their games when they're recognized on a public platform, but the rest of the team is also encouraged to raise their own personal performance bars. Market attention is drawn to the organization, and the entire group strives to make every day, week, month, quarter, or year better than the last.

Regular newsletters can, and should, be used to impart useful data; however, to stop there can be an injustice to the heart of any establishment.

Recognition is a Basic Human Need

Mark is a promising sales representative for a growing insurance firm. His sales leader, Tina, recently cut him loose using the Fledgling Formula. And now, as an independent New Producer, Mark is drumming up leads, following up on quotes, writing contracts...all the things he dreamed he'd be doing, with great success.

Nearly every day, Tina checks in on him. What is Mark working on? How many potential clients did he move through the funnel that day? How many new policies did he write?

And every day, Tina tells Mark how pleased she is with his progress. She emphasizes what a valuable member of the team Mark is, and how positively his work is affecting the company's trajectory.

And yet, all that praise happens within the confines of Marks' cubicle.

Could it be real? Could it be genuine? Or is it just a collection of ego-boosting compliments intended to influence results?

Mark believed he might never know the depth or the sincerity of Tina's accolades...until the company newsletter was distributed.

And there they were in black-and-white: the same words Tina used to describe Mark's work to him. Now they were visible for the entire industry to see.

Newsletters have the potential to serve a number of valuable functions. In addition to the communication of relevant facts, they can:

- introduce new team members
- acknowledge hard work
- track progress
- reward effort
- challenge team members

We cannot assume that the impression of a job well-done is enough for any team member to feel valuable. Personal satisfaction in one's role is essential to long-term success, for sure; however, nothing can replace the loyalty that blossoms from a feeling of being appreciated and recognized—particularly when that recognition is delivered from a public platform.

Feeling valued by others is a fundamental human need. And when humans' needs are met, we see an increase in things like productivity, teamwork, attendance, focus and more.

Remember that what we focus on increases. Focus on your team members' accomplishments, and those accomplishments will multiply!

> *"CULTURE... can't be bought, can't be borrowed, it must be built and nurtured every day."*
>
> *—Coach Davenport*

Coach Davenport's Exercise for You and/or Your Team!

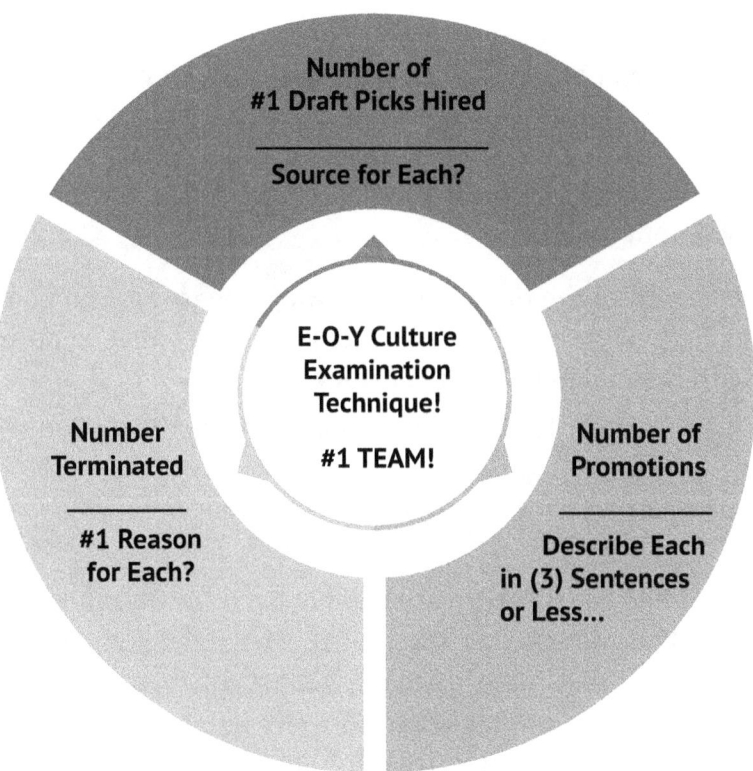

"Measure what Matters and what Matters always IMPROVES!"

—Coach Davenport

"Brett is a dedicated professional whose enthusiasm and passion is second to none. He has helped me better appreciate that we can all get better under coaching but that this takes time and requires us to be purposeful and intentional with everything you do.

I know I will get his very best every time we meet as he is genuinely invested in me as an individual and my success. He has instilled the mindset of being dialed in on all aspects of life and my growth is directly correlated to the time we have spent together.

At the end of the day your reputation is earned, and Coach has helped me create the necessary habits that keep me focused on taking it to the next level."

Dan Toohill, National Mid-Market Sales Director

"I have had the pleasure of knowing Brett for decades. Brett is the true definition of a Leader, Mentor & Coach. Brett is a person that lives life to the fullest. His passion for life and helping others shows in the way he conducts himself both in and outside the boardroom. If you are looking for a Leader/Coach to motivate and bring the best out of your team, Coach D is the man for the job."

Peter Nye, VP of Strategic Accounts,
Morris Group Inc.

"I've known Brett for over 25 years and, having seen his success in several key management positions, I can honestly say there is no better coach! His integrity and charisma have attracted legions of professionals to his Leadership Institute, He knows how to lead by example and hold others accountable for their progress. He's been a loyal friend who always remembers to stay in touch. A truly remarkable person."

Linda Dougherty Borland,
Managing Partner, Insurance Careers

"Coach Davenport was such a great resource for me as I entered the workforce. He opened his network up to me and coached me through a pivotal point in my life. I'm grateful to know him and to have worked with him! He continues to check in on me and genuinely cares about my success as an individual and as a professional."

Maura Bradley, Web3 | sales | executive support

"I have had the pleasure to know Brett for 25 + years. In that timeframe, I have watched Brett set lofty goals of all types and I have watched him exceed each and everyone of them. Brett has the most positive outlook in business and personal of anyone I have known. He is a true leader and has the incredible ability to motivate folks more than they ever imagined possible. His coaching skills and positive attitude are his strengths. You will be that much better if you are fortunate to be coached by Brett."

Anthony R. Cataldo II, President Cataldo Builders Inc.

"I consider myself extremely fortunate to know and have worked with Brett for a number of years. While he came highly recommended when I was looking for an executive coach, the references didn't do him justice. Brett's insights helped me professionally, but more importantly his approach aided me to improve aspects of my personal life. With his guidance, I have been able to get more out of myself than I thought possible. By pushing me and holding me accountable, he has enabled me to become a better person, executive, leader, father, husband, brother and son. Brett has become an important sounding board, confidant and a friend."

Robert Stanley, Head of Client Solutions/COO
Smart USA Company

"Brett Davenport has single-handedly transformed my career as a financial advisor. As a brilliant strategist and problem solver, he's like the Sherlock Holmes of coaches - only more endearing and without the pipe. His loyalty and exceptional listening skills make you feel like you've got your own personal Yoda by your side.

Thanks to Brett over the last 11 years my productivity and success has skyrocketed! THANK YOU COACH!!!!!!!"

Roland Greco, Financial Planner
RG Financial Services

Tip #6
Learn to Earn

Working harder is smarter.

When feral cats or wild bears are fed daily, they lose their drive to hunt. Take that easy food source away, and they will come close to starvation before they attempt to hunt again—and by then, it might be too late. Their physical fitness, their mental acuity, the sharpness of their senses...might be too weakened to support self-reliance.

Humans aren't all that different in this respect.

When you give something to a person, rather than asking them to earn it, you are actually robbing them of the opportunity to better themselves, and to feel the pure exhilaration that comes with personal and professional achievement. They will become dependent on their environment, and that dependency will spread throughout the entire family, workforce or team.

For Their own Good, and the Good of the Organization

Withholding unearned rewards isn't cruel. It isn't unfair. It's not unjust. In fact, it's one of the most caring, generous things you can do for those whom you lead.

- Demonstrate your own work ethic in every task. Even in those cases when no one witnesses your hard work, the result will be evidenced in the ways you interact with others.

- Avoid the temptation to complete tasks for your staff or team members, even though it might be easier to do so.

- Be sure to reward hard work, even if the accomplishments associated with it are not remarkable. The idea here is to impress the ideology that effort is just as valuable as results.

- Resist the "everybody gets a medal" culture. Know that each time everyone is rewarded for the hard work of a few, all are damaged.

- Within your team, work to change perceptions of "winning." A blue ribbon isn't the only way to win. Any group can win with effort, passion, improvement, kindness or sportsmanship.

In the wild, it's only natural for animals to "work smarter, not harder." They must conserve energy, and are therefore highly opportunistic. This contributes to their chances of survival, and so, they're compelled to take what they can get with the least amount of effort possible.

When we are robbed of the privilege to attain that sense of accomplishment, our potential is inhibited. Every time we're *given* something we could have earned for ourselves, we are not only made less self-reliant, we are deprived of the joy that comes with owning something we've worked for.

In a culture where "everyone gets a medal," it can be difficult to maintain a standard that demands earning rather than receiving…and playing all-in rather than simply participating. However, if you guide your team along the higher road, and encourage and reward hard work and merit-based earning, you will compound the value of the experience, as well as the value that's delivered.

Requiring that your team earns every win—and demonstrates that level of integrity in everything they do—might not result in immediate first-place victories. It will, however, practically guarantee countless, significant and crucial wins far into the future…by passionate, independent individuals.

> *"The only way to truly learn and understand is to DO."*
>
> —Coach Davenport

You Can

If you think you are beaten, you are
If you think you dare not, you don't
If you like to win, but think you can't
It's almost a cinch you won't

If you think you'll lose, you've lost;
For out in the world we find
Success begins with a fellow's will'
It's all in the state of mind.

Full many a race is lost
Ere even a step is run,
And many a coward fails,
Ere even his work is begun.

Think big and your deed's will grow.
Think small and you'' fall behind.
Think that you can and you will —
It's all in the state of mind.

If you think you are outclassed, you are;
You've got to think high to rise.
You've got to be sure of yourself
Before you can win a prize.
Life's battles don't always go
To the stronger or faster man'
But sooner or later the man who wins
Is the man who thinks he can.

Unknown

To: The Team I Believe In!
Coach Doug Jr.
#1

Tip #7
Conduct 1:11 Minute Coaching Sessions

Short touchpoints have long-term effects.

If you want to instantly shut off your team's attention and passion, mention the word *Meeting*. Productive meetings do exist, and they must, but calling a meeting every time reassurance, acknowledgment, congratulations, condolences, explanations, or clarifications are in order is not only a waste of valuable time, it's a waste of your team members' interest.

Instead, when you have something important to say to any member of your team, use the 1:11 Minute Coaching Session.

It's quick. It's compact. It's effective. It's unexpected. It's impactful.

And it will not be forgotten.

It's All About the Touchpoints

Building lasting professional relationships isn't about meetings. It's not about scheduled or practiced speeches. Instead, it's all about taking opportunities to interact with your team as it's appropriate, on the fly... whenever you have the chance.

We can talk about taking a minute here or a minute there to make contact with team members. But if we want to add a positive spin (for the most positive possible results), why not think in terms of 1 minute and 11 seconds?

When the number 111 shows itself to you, it can mean a number of things:

- Divine intervention is on the way.
- Positive, high vibration is at work.
- Your genuine, original self is asking to be remembered.
- An angel is present.
- A spiritual message is asking to be delivered.
- Your thoughts are having special relevance to the matter at hand.

And the most significant message that a **1:11** Minute Coaching Session holds:

- "I value your time. I respect your space. But I'm going to take **1** minute and **11** seconds to acknowledge you."

As you go about your day, always be reflecting on what's going on with your team members.

- Has someone lost a loved one? Stick your head into their cubicle, offer your condolences, and ask if there's anything you can do.

- Did someone land a milestone account? Approach them at the water cooler and give them sincere congratulations.

- Was a team member involved in an uncomfortable situation? Stop them in the hallway and let them know you sympathize with them and admire how they handled themselves.

- Did you sense a bit of confusion? Stop by an employee's desk and offer an explanation.

- Has a team member been struggling with self-confidence? Reassure them as you're walking into the office in the morning.

- If someone has been struggling, offer some targeted advice while waiting for the coffee to brew.

Allow time for them to respond; however, avoid turning these 1:11 Sessions into long conversations. The idea is to make a short but lasting impression, while imparting a message that you believe will be pivotal to the recipient's (and the team's) success.

These short touchpoint coaching sessions will allow you to connect with your team as you all go about your day, keeping spirits high and ensuring that every team member feels appreciated, recognized and crucial. And all of this is accomplished while respecting everyone's time.

Embrace the number 111. Notice it when it shows itself to you. And encourage its presence by conducting lots of 1:11 Minute Coaching Sessions.

"If you find yourself in the weeds, go mow the lawn."

—Coach Davenport

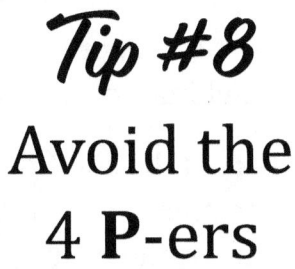

Tip #8
Avoid the 4 **P**-ers

Problem People Poison Potential.

There are two types of people in this world: Those who are part of the solution, and those who are part of the problem. One person can't be part of both. It's an either/or proposition. There is no neutral ground.

Problem **P**eople who **P**oison **P**otential aren't necessarily bad people. Their intentions may be virtuous. However, when you meet someone who is negative, who takes every opportunity to whine, who points their finger at others in blame, or who fills the role of victim as a default...RUN and don't look back.

Your team can only be as strong as its weakest member, and 4 **P**-ers are inevitably the weakest of links. They will bring down the entire operation, robbing even the most purposeful individuals of their potential.

When people are part of the solution, they are positive in thought and action, they show gratitude, they accept responsibility, they uplift the people around them...and they raise the aptitude of the entire team.

Identify 4 P-ers for a Positive, Purposeful Team

Zach was always the last kid picked in gym class, and it wasn't because he couldn't run or jump.

When Zach assisted a goal that was not completed, he blamed the forward for sloppy handling. When he spiked the volleyball into the net, he swore that the net was higher than regulation. When he didn't like the game, he was too tired to play. And when he didn't like the team he was placed on, he refused to play all-out.

*(I'm confident that if you've ever met a 4 **P**-er, you could add many more scenarios of what Zach might say or do...)*

What's more, whatever team Zach ended up on usually lost. His whining and finger-pointing sparked arguments among his team mates, and while they were busy bringing each other down, the opponent took that opportunity to rocket ahead with team work and a spirit of cooperation.

Whether you're making sure that you're part of the solution (and not the problem) or you're looking for people who are part of the solution to add to your team, it can help to practice recognizing positive behaviors, as well as the behaviors of **P**roblem **P**eople who **P**oison **P**otential.

If you notice these qualities and habits from any given person, back away and run quickly in the other direction:

- dwelling on mistakes of the past...especially when those mistakes were made by other people
- making excuses for their poor choices
- complaining about tasks they don't enjoy
- bringing others down in an attempt to raise themselves up
- blaming others for undesirable outcomes
- failing to give credit to others...but taking lots of it for themselves
- spreading feelings of negativity...sometimes (or many times) without saying a word
- chattering with a victim mentality
- maintaining a poor outlook for the future

You can identify 4 **P**-ers by analyzing their behavior, or by listening to them speak. Ironically, this can be detected in less time than the precious positive 1:11 minute coaching session in Tip #7.

Plus, your intuition will also work to identify them. If you've ever gotten a bad feeling about someone, but had no evidence to back it up, you might have ignored that feeling and continued to interact with them. Chances are you also learned later on that those initial feelings were speaking to you—or screaming at you—to stay away.

Your intuition is rarely wrong, and 4 **P**-ers are ALWAYS a problem.

> *"ABR....*
> *Always Be Recruiting."*
> *—Coach Davenport*

Tip #9
Perform a 52-Week Look-Back

Attention to detail in any self-assessment promotes personal and professional growth.

When we think of a performance review, we often think of a meeting between an employee and his or her boss(es), in which all the drudgery of the past year is dug up, while everyone struggles to remember what that team member's accomplishments might have been.

It doesn't have to be that way!

In fact, a 52-Week Look-Back should be something you conduct by yourself, for yourself, for your personal and professional growth.

A Yearly Review, but More Manageable & Time Efficient

Robert wanted the coming year to be his best sales year yet, so he sat down in his office with a tablet and a pencil. He would make a list of all the significant things he did last year—including his accomplishments and his disappointments, his victories and his poor choices.

He drummed his fingers on the desk. He scratched the names of a few accounts he landed on his paper. He remembered that time he allowed the competition to grab up a big client. But the details were fuzzy. He couldn't quite remember the chronological order of things, or the events that led up to each outcome.

Robert couldn't help but think that his yearly self-review had resulted in more doubt and questions than clarity.

Next door, Angela opened her 52-Week Self-Assessment Journal and reviewed not only her triumphs and failures along the way, but developed a plan for the coming year, based on last year's progression, setbacks and growth.

In business, sports, non-profits and more, yearly accomplishments are viewed as barometers of past performance *and* future plans. A review of the previous year is necessary to foster growth in the next. However, it can be difficult to recall the events of the last 52 weeks if they have not been chronicled in an orderly fashion. Just try to remember everything that happened last year in one sitting. You're sure to miss some pretty important events—events that could be invaluable teaching experiences for the future, both personally and professionally.

You should be journaling already, as suggested in Tip #4. Now add a weekly review to that journal so that at the end of the year, you can refer back to 52 bite-size appraisals of where you've been (instead of one muddy memory of a year gone by).

Include things like:

- goals that were reached, and why
- goals that were not reached, and why
- great impressions made by positive people
- poor impressions made by 4 **P**-ers
- valuable connections you made
- connections you made that led nowhere (or backward)
- your most satisfied customers, fans or affiliates...the people you pleased
- people who were disappointed

- situations that could have been improved with more wisdom, action or thought
- circumstances that were beyond your control
- failures that were teaching moments
- victories you'd like to duplicate or expand upon over the next 52 weeks

It's easy to believe we'll remember all the things that have happened to us, personally and professionally. But in truth, days go slow and years go fast. One momentous event will take the place of others, and as our focus shifts, so will our memories.

So keep track, on a weekly basis, of what happened on your way to reaching your goals. Then set aside time to review and use that information to build your growth strategy for the next year!

> *"Efficient or ineffective—the choice is easy, and it separates winners from survivors."*
>
> *—Coach Davenport*

Tip #10
Practice R³ for Maximum Performance

Rest, Relaxation, and Reflection multiply potential to the third power.

What's in a vacation? On the surface, it's valuable time spent with family, the privilege of unwinding and looking after your health…as well as time away from work and a backlog that will take weeks to catch up on. Not to mention all the mice that will be playing while the cat's away.

Whoa, there.

If, as a leader, you experience anxiety at the mere mention of taking a vacation, or you don't believe you can afford to do so, then it's time to take an inventory of what you're really losing by failing to use your vacation time.

How to Turn Vacation Time into Team Growth

When we talk about taking vacation time as leaders, that doesn't mean we're taking our laptops to the beach or answering our phones while hiking the Adirondacks. What it does mean is that we're using the time off to reflect on what we want, what we've achieved, and where we're going.

There's no rule against thinking about our leadership roles while on vacation; there is, however, a rule about avoiding vacation because we can't stop thinking about our leadership roles.

Here are a few pieces of advice for the vacation you're about to schedule:

- **Trust your leadership skills.** You are a leader who has used the Fledgling Formula to create New Producers who are independent, purposeful and team oriented. You are a professional mentor and manager, not a hand-holder or a babysitter. That means your time away is essential to the growing independence of those whom you lead. So quit worrying. NOT being there from time to time is part of your leadership responsibilities.
- **In order to be an effective leader, you've got to master the technique of stepping outside your bubble and looking in.** This can also be

called Big-Picture Thinking, and it brings to light all sorts of circumstances that would otherwise go unnoticed. I trust that your leadership role is a big part of your life, and while on vacation you'll have plenty of time to step back and reflect on how your life is unfolding, and how your leadership role is contributing to the realization of all your life's goals. This far-back view enables you to respond instead of react, and to see the big picture without being distracted by "the small stuff."

- **Vacation unlocks your creative and risk-taking potential, which will then overflow into your work.** These two elements are almost always underrated, but without the ability and the drive to "think outside the box," you can only be a run-of-the-mill leader, at best. So go ahead and paint that pottery, or hang glide, or pick the biggest water slide—it will be good for business.

- **Your team members need time off just as much as you do.** By clocking out (and returning refreshed), you're demonstrating the value of vacations.

So you can go on like you've been, avoiding vacations because you just don't have the time, or because the team can't live without you...or any other number of reasons. You can continue to just survive, hanging on by a thread, tired and drained, delivering less than what you know you're capable of.

Or, you can perform with efficiency and wisdom... to WIN.

> *"If we are wildly successful professionally, but we fail personally... we fail."*
>
> —Coach Davenport

Coach Davenport's Challenge to You and/or Your Team!

Please invest the time today to create your successful unified and healthy vacation process... Then go experience it!

#1

_____
_____
_____
_____
_____
_____
_____
_____

"As a top sales performer transitioning to a sales leadership role, I was provided the opportunity to work with Coach Davenport. I will admit a level of skepticism at the onset. I thought I knew a lot, that I had been performing to my highest level, that I knew how to get the most out of my teams—I had it figured out. Boy was I wrong. Brett has enabled me to think bigger, to envision a higher level for me and those around me and, most importantly, has worked with me to develop the path to get there with a measurable, known goal line. If the story ended there, it would be a success. But Brett's gift is to continually help you challenge yourself, to once again think bigger, to set and attain even higher goals, to major in the majors, to hold yourself and those around you accountable. That has made him a great mentor and a key element of my professional success.

That said, I have equally valued Brett's friendship and the time we have spent learning about each other as people. Brett is a family man and places a high value on helping you succeed professionally while at the same time having a fulfilled personal life—it is impossible to truly have one without the other. I consider Brett a coach, mentor, friend and the secret sauce to my professional and personal success.

If you are looking to take it to the next level or if you think you have it all figured out, Brett is the best in the business and can help you get to places you have a hard time conceiving today."

Nick McParland, Divisional Vice President

"Brett makes leaders better by holding them accountable for what they decide to do. Plain and simple and powerful."

Ami Tully Lotka, Owner and President, Maximum Impact Partners, Inc

"Coach Davenport has helped me develop both personally and professionally. He has helped me set goals, achieve them, and learn leadership skills while doing so. He genuinely cares about my family and me even though the base of our relationship is professional. He is always available as member of my team in every way that matters."

Bob Weisse, CFA, CFP®, Chief Investment Officer at Heritage Financial Services

"Brett brings great energy, insight and leadership to every encounter. He becomes a key resource to everyone he comes into contact with. He learns other peoples 'why' and dedicates himself to supporting their cause by building a clear strategy for winning. He spots the details that others overlook and takes the time to celebrate the wins that are sometimes hidden. Coach pushes the team to reach for great over good by introducing stretch goals that test leadership skills. Thanks, Coach!"

Robert Nixon, MBA, CFP®, CLU®, EA, Senior Vice President at InspereX

"Brett repeatedly participated in learning with an extremely positive attitude and open mind. He is eager to learn everything he can to further develop and polish his skills and abilities. Brett also became a fantastic role model for others in his course. His ability to interact with people effectively, communicate his ideas passionately, and handle himself as a professional under extreme pressure are just a few of the qualities Brett demonstrated on a consistent basis. We admired his passion for life and learning as well as his empathy for others. As a leader, Brett is someone that I would definitely enjoy working for and would also feel very comfortable referring to any business looking for a integral team member, coach or speaker."

Leslie English, Communications Division General Manager at United Radio and Former Dale Carnegie Franchise Owner

"Having known Brett for over five years, he has always been an enthusiastic advocate who embodies the leadership qualities he preaches. In my experience, he will never cease to encourage you, and will support without fail; however, he will also challenge you, in order to make your best better! Brett is always the consummate professional. He is caring, funny and likely to send warm birthday wishes to you and your family members before you've even gotten out of bed. Congrats on your 3rd book, "Steadfast Leadership"!!"

Jonathan A. Moyer, CFP®, Wealth Advisor
Carson Wealth

Tip #11
Tear Down Silos, Build Bridges

No one can flourish in the darkness, in the quiet, with all their own junk piling up on them.

What is a specialty? On a team, you have forwards, defenders and goalies. You have outfielders, infielders, pitchers and catchers. You have linemen, linebackers, tight ends, receivers, running backs, safeties, centers and quarterbacks.

In an office, you have human resources, customer service, accounts payable, accounts receivable, reception and office manager.

In a family, you have children, parents, grandparents and pets. Maybe even aunts, uncles, cousins, in-laws and neighbors.

And if each specialty, department or classification operated on its own, without support and without giving support, in its own solitude—in its own silo—would there even be a team, business or family?

If each specialty operates in a silo (or an enclosed space where no light gets in), no communication can be heard, and all of their own junk just continues to pile on top of them, is the accomplishment of goals even possible? Don't you have a siloed operation that simply cannot grow?

If, on the other hand, those silos are disassembled, all the "stuff" is allowed to spread out, and bridges are built from one specialty pile to the next, then we're in business.

Connected Piles, not Silos, to Stimulate Growth

Sometimes silos are put up as defense mechanisms. Or, they are built because they seem to promote focus. Other times, those silos have been in existence for so long that operating any other way seems foreign.

No matter how they got there, they've got to be torn down—and as a leader, it's your job to make that happen.

Here's how:

- **Set common goals.** When every specialty is working toward one big-picture, collective goal (with the purpose provided by individual and departmental goals), everyone wins.

- **Promote communication.** The idea that we don't need to know the functions and procedures of other specialties is an unworkable concept. No team or operation can grow without a "big picture" view.

- **Save the competition for your competitors.** A little competition among team members isn't a bad thing; it drives everyone to improve. However, when the competition among specialties within one organization is more vigorous than it is with the organization's outside competitors, growth will be stunted.

- **Make decisions with synergy.** When one specialty is left out of any equation, nothing adds up. That's why every time there's a decision to be made, all involved should be consulted with, or at least considered.

- **Establish empathy.** When one specialty doesn't understand what others go through on a daily basis, it can be easy to lose sight of long-term, organization-wide goals. Tear down silos through education and new experiences.

- **Modify language.** "That's not my job," "I don't know anything about that," "Not my department," "Why do you need to know that?" "It's always been done this way," and, "If it doesn't pertain to my job, I'm not interested," are keeping departments siloed, minds closed and goals unattainable. Each statement along these lines is a brick in a silo.

Bridges built between specialties open clear channels for communication, understanding, empathy and common goals. Without any of these elements, a unit made of a number of departments simply cannot survive.

So tear down those silos, and carry each brick, one-by-one, to build the bridges that will connect every person to every specialty on your team.

> *"We learn much more by listening vs lecturing."*
>
> *—Coach Davenport*

Tip #12
Eliminate the *Perfect* Enemy

The high cost of perfection is the loss of learning, growth and authentic relationships.

What's the problem with perfection? Particularly when you're charged with setting examples for those you lead?

Perfection ensures a quality product, right? It increases productivity and efficiency, right? And reputation...it advances that.

Right...?

Perfection distracts us while opportunities pass by. It convinces us that we must wait until we're "ready," which never really happens. It's not an asset. It is a roadblock—a hindrance—to all the things you could be accomplishing right now.

Perfect is the Enemy of Good

Michelle is a self-proclaimed perfectionist. Her office is neat and organized. Procedure and protocol are of the utmost importance in her department. The only risks she takes are ones that others have tried first or ones that she can virtually guarantee will result in professional and personal achievement. Anything less would be an embarrassment, or a waste of time.

She demands the same of her team. There isn't much freedom for being innovative, and "the way we've always done it" is the culture.

Michelle is driven by the fear of failure.

Compared to Michelle, Kevin is a bit of a renegade. He likes to try new procedures and test new strategies. He tells his team that he's taking them on "little adventures," and encourages them to do the same. When these experiments don't work out—if money is lost or a customer is disappointed—they make reparations and move on, with mental notes about how they'll never do that again, or how they'll make adjustments next time.

Kevin's team members are enthusiastic. They have great respect for their leader. They feel they have the freedom to explore their own talents to be the best they can be, for the common good of the organization.

Michelle's team, on the other hand, rides the rails. They experience anxiety when suggesting something new, and so they rarely do. They know their leader is unlikely to agree to step off the beaten path. And so, the fear of consequence is real.

When the time comes to promote from within, Kevin is a shoe-in. It is evident to upper management that he does not demand perfection from himself or his team; he only demands learning and growth...both of which lead to profit.

As humans, we can't possibly perform at the top of our games if we're subjecting ourselves to perpetual self-judgment. The stress that results from fearing anything less than perfection weighs on us, physically, mentally, emotionally and spiritually. And when we're in that state, we cannot be expected to lead with any level of mastery.

- **Stop waiting until you're "ready."** The best leaders move forward in spite of doubt and fear, correcting along the way.
- **Understand that perfection is fear in disguise.** We have come to recognize perfection as a personality trait, when really, it's nothing more than an excuse for avoiding risk.

- **Step back and look at the toll perfection in leadership might be taking on your team.** You are their example for what they should and shouldn't do. When you play it safe, so will they—and this is *not* the path to victory.

- **Instead of focusing on making everything perfect, focus on cultivating your problem-solving and mediation skills.** These are valuable abilities that will serve your team more than the demand for perfection.

- **Recognize how much you've been missing by keeping your head buried in a current project, "perfecting" it.** First, know that it will never be "perfect." There is no such thing. Second, know that completing tasks with integrity and keeping an eye open for opportunities is the "perfect" plan.

Perfectionism, micro-management...whatever you want to call it, is not serving you as a leader. It's a distraction; a roadblock that must be removed if you're ever going to perform at your maximum personal and professional potential.

> *"Remember, it isn't about how much you wrote, it's that you wrote!"*
>
> *—Coach Davenport*

Tip #13
Call the Play

The most damaging external criticism is delivered in hindsight.

When a decision is made that doesn't work as well as expected, and someone who was silent during the decision-making process criticizes that decision, what does that mean?

Does it mean that person is interested in improvement and growth? Does it mean that they're supporting the one they're criticizing?

None of the above. More often, it means they're suffering from a case of envy, and they're leveling to make themselves feel (and appear) more competent than the one they're criticizing. Had they genuinely been concerned with the outcome, or if they had anything valuable to contribute, they would have done so before the call was made.

Monday Morning Quarterbacks are toxic to your leadership, and to the entire team. Similarly, adopting the role of Monday Morning Quarterback can turn your team against you.

You've got to have the nerve and the integrity to decide whether to get involved early and assume accountability for the outcome, or stand back and allow lessons to be learned, offering support without criticism.

Late Calls are Safe Calls

The Woodchucks' season opener was a breeze. The pitcher only allowed three hits, all of which were left on base for a shut-out game. It was a pure slug fest, with two homeruns, four triples, a number of doubles and too many singles to count. Coach Somers knew he had made some bad calls, like giving the steal sign to his slowest runner and calling a bunt after the second strike. Nobody seemed to notice, though. The fans were giddy. The players were celebratory.

The next game didn't go as well. The opposing team was of a completely different caliber, and they had the Woodchucks covering every inch of the outfield... without much success. Even though the 'Chucks had taken a hard loss, Coach was happy with the calls he had made. He brought out the best in every player and as a team, they put themselves on the board. However, not everyone saw it like Coach Somers did. The criticism started as soon as the game ended. The players were grumbling, throwing around a variety of "should haves." The fans were shouting insults. Even the newspaper article the next day cast a shadow on the coach and his team. "Somers Sends Woodchucks to Slaughter" was the headline.

How could this be? How could he do everything his decades of experience told him was right, with cheering fans and willing players, only to learn they didn't agree with any of it after it was all over?

Being a leader involves taking risks. It involves making decisions that most others aren't willing to make. And the same reason that everyone is not leadership material is the same reason they're not speaking up until there's something to criticize. They don't have the nerve, experience, grit, talent, passion...whatever it might be...to stand at the lead, be vulnerable and stick their necks out for the good of everyone involved.

Be cautious of Monday Morning Quarterbacks. Check yourself when it comes to this type of behavior, because true leaders don't bring up the rear.

"Hindsight is 20/20, but Foresight is Leadership!"
—Coach Davenport

Yes YOU Can!

#1

Tip #14
Concentrate on Cadence

Cadence is crucial; duration, not so much.

In order to produce predictable results, you must create an environment in which there are continual catalysts. From consistency is born consistency. From chaos is born chaos. And when leadership touchpoints are delivered with a rhythmic cadence, the result is beautiful music.

One of a leader's most important responsibilities is creating an atmosphere of diligence that isn't exhausting or frustrating to those expected to contribute. And contrary to popular belief, the frequency of meetings isn't the problem—it's the content...and even more significant, the length of those meetings.

Remember that a "meeting" can have two implications: A) a long, drawn-out, or exhaustive gathering with a complex or convoluted meaning or B) a brief encounter that is expected *and* impactful. When you meet someone, it's a meeting. Only in modern office environments has the meeting come to be maligned, thanks to a lack of respect for people's time.

Aren't you ready to get back to the root of the "meeting"? When it was meaningful, and something to celebrate?

Cadence Breeds Consistency

When leaders establish a cadence in regard to the touchpoints they make with their team, that consistency and predictability carry over to every touchpoint those team members create with the customer, the fan base, the public...whomever they're interacting with.

And as we know, a crucial factor in building trust is constancy. Sporadic contact or unpredictable interactions simply cannot breed trust.

As a conscious leader, you can establish cadence with:
- regularly scheduled performance reviews
- goal progress checkups
- monthly, quarterly and yearly debriefings
- team performance reviews

- planning for upcoming monthly, quarterly and yearly goals
- coaching to resolve "**A**reas **O**f **D**evelopment" and enhance strengths
- individual check-ins

And to reiterate, all of these team cadence touchpoints should be scheduled in advance, with attention toward efficient communication and a respect for everyone's time.

It can be a challenge to move from the types of meetings we've all come to dread toward this compact leadership cadence model. You can start by:

- **Do away with the boardroom whenever possible.** Entering a room, taking a seat, closing the door…all contribute to the idea that we've got to be there for a while. Try a middle-of-the-office or a middle-of-the-court stand-up meeting instead. The huddle isn't just for game time. It's for debriefing, planning and goal setting too.
- **Stick to a precise schedule in each meeting.** This will help maintain focus and move everyone through the agenda (even if it's only one or two items) quickly. These agendas should be duplicated in all the same types of meetings.
- **Steer around rabbit trails.** Meetings can become long and laborious when small talk is tolerated. Stick to the topic and move through with efficiency.

- **Keep it positive.** Just because your leadership cadence touchpoints are short and to-the-point doesn't mean they have to be abrupt or lacking emotion. Strive to ensure that everyone leaves each meeting with the excitement they need to keep up the rhythm.

By concentrating on cadence in your leadership, you can provide your team with the confidence they need to move forward steadily, knowing that everyone is being fueled and supported by a consistent flow of purpose, encouragement and objectives. There won't be time for anyone to slip out of rhythm, because another beat will be coming along…just in time.

"Talent unused is worthless, talent untapped is priceless, let's tap— potential with a consistent cadence."

—Coach Davenport

Tip #15
Execute the Plan

Don't kill the business plan, execute it!

Why do we write business plans? In many cases, we write them because the bank wants to see one before they'll loan us money, or because a manufacturer we're supplying requests it. We might even use it to acquaint new team members with our organizations—but the question eventually comes up: Are you putting that business plan to good use? Too often, the business plans we create out of obligation are left to die, all alone in abandoned folders that no one visits or consults. They're essentially killed, when they should, in fact, be executed.

Therein lies the problem: Those business plans contain everything you need to guide you to the type of success you're envisioning. When you forget why you're in business, it will remind you. When you lose sight of your goals, there it is. And when you forget what you told investors, financial institutions, affiliates and team members about your business, it's all right there, in the business plan.

The business plan is a rich resource that has gone largely overlooked.

Now is the time to see it...and to execute.

Getting the Most out of Writing, and Revisiting, that Business Plan

I know that creating a business plan is sometimes an afterthought—something you might do because someone is demanding it, or because it's "protocol." However, if you can immerse yourself in the process of writing it, you will not only discover things about you and your business, you will open your mind to possibilities by putting yourself in an if/then pattern of thinking.

So many leaders discover an abundance of great things while writing their business plans—and then they assume that's the end of it. When in fact, they can rediscover more good things simply by putting that business plan's strategy into action on a daily basis.

Here are a few scenarios in which your business plan can lead your team to victories, large and small:

- If you're feeling inadequate, or nervous about an upcoming challenge, the **Achievements** portion will be there to remind you that you're more than capable. You've put in the work and you've got this!

- Your **Concept** will help you to remember how enthusiastic you were when your organization was brand new. It will remind you what a great idea you had—and now that you know even more about the market and your competencies, you can put that great idea to practical use.

- When you lose sight of how you can expand income streams, you can refer to the **Profit** section of your business plan, to revisit the possibilities you once saw. Now, with your expanded knowledge, you can take that insight and sharpen it.

- Your **Marketing Strategies** can remind you about whom you're serving, and the different ways you can connect with them—just in case you start to feel that you're on the inside looking out, longing for objectivity.

- It can be easy to forget about what makes you stand out from your competitors, but your business plan's **Positioning** section will not only refresh your memory, it will remind you about your purpose, and how you can put it to work in unique ways.

That business plan may have started out as obligatory, but that doesn't mean it must go on to be impractical, or irrelevant.

Write that plan. Execute that plan. And trust it to be the living, breathing lifeblood of your organization.

"Business planning is overused, but grossly under-utilized."

—Coach Davenport

Coach Davenport's Exercise for You and/or Your Team!

Please clearly memorialize your #1 strategic action for each of these annual opportunistic periods...

- Fast Start (FS)
- Summer Sales Success (SSS)
- Strong Finish (SF)

#1 Strategy to Capture Market Share!

#1 TEAM!

#1 – Fast Start (FS)

_____
_____
_____
_____
_____

#1 — Summer Sales Success (SSS)

_____
_____
_____
_____
_____
_____

#1 — Strong Finish (SF)

_____
_____
_____
_____
_____
_____

"Coach Davenport has helped our executive team to work on our business and not just in our business. He has helped us think through many strategic decisions and held us accountable each month for making progress toward our company goals. His leadership experience has provided us with a valuable perspective when working through "people" challenges in our organization. He has helped us to understand some key metrics in our business that need to be tracked and monitored that has led to an increase in our growth."

Bobby Schneider, CFP®, Advisor & Director of Operations, C.I.G. Private Wealth Management

"Brett is a true inspiration! I can count on one hand the number of people with his focused energy. I thoroughly enjoyed his coaching book, so much so that I asked him to present to my classroom. The kids loved it! If only we could have his optimism and spark to motivate my classroom students every day! Not to mention, he is an upstanding community member who volunteers his time and his family is a testament to his motivational skills."

Deborah Gleason-Rielly, Analytical Problem Solver, Educator, Registered Nurse, Writer

"I have known Brett for several years now and he has always been true to his work and strive for nothing short of excellence when working with his clients. The rapport I have developed with Brett has made it a privilege to know him. The professionalism and expertise he brings to the table along with his commitment to his clients makes him a Steadfast Leader!"

Loraine McMillan, Entrepreneur

"I have had the great privilege of working with Brett for several years now and I can sincerely say he has made a profound difference in both my personal and professional lives. Brett continually reinforces the importance of staying focused on what matters most. His "steps vs leaps" approach combined with his high standards of accountability have helped me accomplish more than I thought was possible.

Brett's passion is beyond reproach. He has a unique ability to drill down and identify the most important factors in being successful. His optimism, enthusiasm and positive attitude are truly contagious (spend a few minutes with him and you'll know what I mean).

His advice and guidance have been priceless. If you want to take your career to the next level, then Coach is your guy. If you think you're good—he'll make you better. He will take a genuine interest in your success as he has mine and for that I will forever be grateful to him."

Mark Lowbridge, Divisional Vice President

"I am so grateful to have gained Brett into my network at a fairly young age, working for him during a few very developmental years in my life. Brett's passion to help others in coaching and leadership is a genuine piece of his DNA, not just his business, and it bleeds into everything he does. He brings his coaching attitude and mindset into every interaction; leaving you with a sense of control on your circumstances, pride in accomplishments, understanding of the actions you must take to get where you'd like to go and the confidence to do so. Brett is extremely easy and enjoyable to communicate with, always making you feel his top priority when speaking one on one. From his demeanor, you can tell he truly cares for others and is invested in those around him regardless of whether you are a client or personal relationship of his. Or even a compete stranger for that matter! I would highly recommend him to anyone—those just starting their careers, established professionals still looking for more, or even those interested in taking things in their personal lives to the next level. I truly admire his energy and enthusiasm for life and am thankful for the relationship we've kept over the years. I always look forward to catching up with Brett a few times a year!"

Mikaela Anderson Wilson, Executive Assistant to Chief Revenue Officer at Deepwatch

"From my very first meeting with Brett, his enthusiasm, passion and desire to see me succeed was undeniable. And since then, he has guided me through a clear roadmap to success that is purposeful and intentional. I look forward to working with him for many years to come."

Rebecca Dehainaut, Regional Vice President

"I was first introduced to Brett back in 2017 from a colleague who's work habits and success I admired. Looking back these 6 years I can easily say that the decision to bring Brett in as part of "my Team" has been one of the very best investments I've ever made. If you are contemplating this same decision, don't hesitate to reach out to me and I'd gladly share the many reasons why I think so highly of Brett and the wonderful work that he does."

Kuosen Fung, Certified Financial Planner at
RBC Wealth Management

"I had been away from personal sales production for over ten years when I met Brett. He quickly diagnosed my strengths and areas of development, then put me on a simple, yet highly efficient & effective plan to maximize my God given talents! His encouragement and ability to have me focus on only the "most important thing" each month has helped me tremendously. The changes in my production, attitude, and overall enjoyment of my role, I attribute in great part to Coach D. I wouldn't want to be on this journey without him."

Tom Skelley, Wealth Advisor
Carson Wealth

Tip #16
Be a Thermostat

Don't just read the temperature, regulate it.

Let's think about the differences between a thermometer and a thermostat.

A thermometer tells you what the temperature is. A thermostat tells the temperature what to be.

A thermometer reports the facts. A thermostat utilizes facts to create a comfortable environment.

A thermometer sits by idly while temperatures soar or plummet, out of control. A thermostat takes control and solves the problem before extremes are felt.

A thermometer reacts. A thermostat responds.

As a leader, you are far more valuable to your team when you act as a thermostat. As a thermometer, you assume a role of helplessness. You might state the problem, or the discomfort, and then do little more than raise the mercury and cause alarm.

When you operate as a Thermostat Leader, you are in control. You are a problem-solver. You work to manage all the extremes of working with a team.

Respond and Regulate, like a Thermostat

Jim is the manager of Sales Team A, which has taken on three new salespeople in the past quarter. Every time a new team member enters the scene, the atmosphere of the department shifts. While producers work to figure out how each new recruit ticks, each new producer endeavors to learn where they fit in, and what's expected of them.

Tensions flare. Sales philosophies clash. Veteran team members feel threatened by the performance of the newcomers. The new recruits feel judged and avoid making decisions.

Jim feels like he's losing control. Every day, he can be heard making statements like, "It's getting tense in there," "These people just can't get along," and, "I have no control over this new team."

A similar situation has unfolded with Gail's team—Team B. However, the result couldn't be more distinct from Jim's. The entire Team B, new recruits included, is working together to fill each other's gaps and to achieve a common goal. In just three months' time, they have exceeded last quarter's numbers.

Jim claims that Gail's new producers are of a different caliber than his. They have more experience, they're more agreeable...and many, many similar claims.

But the real difference? Gail can be heard saying of her Team B: "Let's talk about how that made you feel," "Let's see what we can do about that territory overlap," and, "Here's the goal, here's what's standing in the way, and here's what we can do about moving forward as a team."

Gail detects problems within before they balloon out of control. Jim allows those problems to swell, and then feels helpless in regulating poor morale that has expanded beyond his control.

As a leader, it's your job to detect fluctuations in your team's ambient "temperature" and address those fluctuations before it becomes too hot or too cold to regulate. Stay in-tune with the needs of your team. Listen intently for signs of unrest. Promote focus and always look for ways to check in and to encourage.

Respond, rather than react, and watch as trust in you becomes your team's new normal.

"Compensation drives behavior, be strategic in your planning each year."

—Coach Davenport

STEADFAST LEADERSHIP...

As a LEADER, it is necessary to know your TEAM's Strengths & Areas of Development so you can BEST figure out how to WIN on the "fill in the blank" of play!!

When an organization is struggling, losing its way or trying to find their foundation again... it takes time, patience and STEADFAST LEADERSHIP!!

Steadfast Leadership—can be defined as:

- PURPOSE DRIVEN MINDSET
- A Healthy CADENCE of Vision
- Crystal Clear CLARITY of Mission
- Unwavering POSITIVE Body Language
- Character to OWN the Results
- 100% Commitment to Personal & Professional GROWTH
- Hungry Passion to See PEOPLE Reach/Exceed their POTENTIAL
- Confident Presence that CHALLENGES are Welcome and Required to ACHIEVE SUCCESS
- ACCOUNTABLE... Period!

Competition is always MOTIVATING, but sometimes the obvious victory doesn't happen the way it was forecasted or prepared for... but any SEASONED LEADER knows that LESSONS LEARNED are the BEST GIFT in LIFE!!

Finally, what I've experience over 59 years is that, most often, the SWEETEST Victories are the ones with the smallest margin or WON in OT... with Grit, Determination, Teamwork and an "EXPECT TO WIN" ATTITUDE!

Tip #17
Know Your Brand's Position

Know with whom, and for whom, you're competing.

Your brand isn't just your logo, or your product, or your service. Instead, it's an accumulation of the feelings and opinions the public has about your organization. The public has those perceptions; however, you are the one responsible for giving them the information they need to shape those perceptions.

Your brand is much like your reputation: You make the decisions that lead other people to form beliefs about you.

All of this means you have choices about how your brand will be received in relation to all the others sharing space with it. Of course, there will be opinions that go against what you're intending to build; but for the most part, the public's reality of what your organization is about will be shaped based on the decisions you make, the values you demonstrate, the way you treat people, the way you respond to a variety of circumstances...and so much more.

What do you want your brand to stand for? How do you want it to be perceived, and therefore received? What do you want people to say about it? And what position will it occupy in relation to its competition?

Answer these questions, and you will find yourself positioned in one of three places:

- Basic Economy
- Main Cabin
- First Class

The choice is yours.

How will your Brand Take Flight?

When we think of brands, we might think of big companies like Nike and Coca-Cola. The truth is that almost anything can be a brand: a business, a team, a club, a movement...even a person. So no matter what you're intending to brand, you've got to decide whom you want to serve and how you want to be perceived in the circle they belong to.

If you fly on a regular basis, you'll be able to appreciate the airplane metaphor I've already alluded to.

- In **Basic Economy**, there's no advanced seat selection. The seats recline a few inches (if at all), and leg room is not an amenity you'll experience. There are baggage restrictions and limited overhead storage. You will board after the rest of the passengers have been seated. The tickets for these seats are cheap, and everyone on the plane knows it. Good luck getting peanuts.

- In the **Main Cabin**, you might have the luxury of choosing your seat. You'll enjoy dedicated overhead storage, and a comfortable amount of leg room. There will be entertainment and complimentary snacks.

- In **First Class**, you will board first. You might enjoy gourmet food, champagne, a pillow, slippers, a blanket…all with personal service from a dedicated flight attendant. Seats recline way back and leg room is abundant. Work space is provided, with amenities for privacy, silence or personalized entertainment.

How will the public perceive your brand? Cheap? Cut-Rate? Uncomfortable? Average? Simply Acceptable?

Or Top-Notch? The Best-of-the-Best? First-Class?

The choice is yours. What kind of impressions do you want to make on the public? And what kind of experiences do you want anyone who comes in contact with your brand to have?

If you aspire to be known as a first-class brand, remember that for passengers, upgrades at check-in are complimentary—they never cost a thing, but the experience is always priceless.

"Push your Potential with Purpose!"

—Coach Davenport

Tip #18
Win with Flawless Follow-Up

A string of flawless follow-ups makes a conversation. Meaningful conversation builds enduring relationships.

There are a number of situations in which follow-up is warranted. After interviews, one-on-one encounters, board meetings, performances, customer contacts and so much more require that communication not be dropped, but furthered in the interest of building relationships.

And if you're in this to win, it can't be just any old follow-up. It's got to be customized, targeted, relevant, unforgettable and act as a catalyst for future interactions.

Relationships can be complicated. Any time two unique individuals or entities come together, countless factors are at play. There are personalities, opinions, motives, intentions, wishes, beliefs, histories, filters and more. Under the best circumstances, both parties share the same goals. Under *most* circumstances, there will be elements that require conversation and compromise.

Everything after the first encounter is a follow-up, and each follow-up should enhance knowledge, build in intensity, and highlight what's at stake for the long term.

That's why every follow-up must be carefully strategized and implemented...so it's utterly flawless.

A String of Strategic Successes, in the Form of Follow-Ups

The first step to follow-up is setting it up. During an initial encounter with anyone, give them points to think about for the next few days. Challenge the status quo. Give them some homework, or ways they can prove to themselves that what you're saying is wholly legitimate. In other words, strategize this meeting so there will be plenty to talk about during your first follow-up.

The most controllable facet of follow-up is remembering to do it. Sounds simple, right? Who could forget to check in with the people who hold the future of your organization in their hands? It's easier to forget than you might think. After every first meeting, whether you hit it out of the park or you made only minimal progress, send yourself a text or email as a reminder to follow up in a few days.

A lot can happen in a short amount of time. The other prospective deal they were talking to could fall through. Their viewpoint may change after having some time to think about what you presented. They could have more questions, or may have additional objections that need attention. No matter what, remember to be there so that no thought is left incomplete or question is left unanswered.

Treat every follow-up as a conversation in a string of conversations to come. Know that there will be follow-ups to your follow-ups and that you have the responsibility to plan for what's next in every situation. You can prepare the people you interact with to expect the follow-up by always leaving one part of your interaction unresolved. Always know, and leave others with the impression, that there's more to talk about.

Also, understand that "everyone" is texting and emailing to follow up with the people you want to build relationships with. Pick up the phone. It makes a lasting impression, and gives you the opportunity to use tone and inflection to fully communicate, rather than risking a crucial connection missing your point, or underestimating your energy or commitment.

And finally, remember to make the follow-up "all about them." Has the information you provided helped them? What more can you do? Look at what you found since your last meeting!

Never forget that a conversation doesn't have to happen in one sitting. It can be strung out over time, as long as the communication is coherent, relevant and connected. Keep those conversations going, and win with the relationships that result.

"The fortune is in the follow-UP"

—Coach Davenport

Tip #19
Empower Your Executive Assistant

For more effective time management, empower the one who manages your time.

Your personal assistant, executive assistant, right-hand man or woman...has the ability to make your work life (and beyond) run either like a well-oiled machine or a broken-down rattletrap. If you've experienced both, you know how isolated the extremes can be.

Not only is your assistant responsible for taking care of all the things you don't have time for, he or she is responsible for taking care of all the things that make your success possible. It can be easy to forget that the things they handle are just as crucial as the things you do. For instance, if you land a meeting with a high-profile potential client, you'll never secure the account without the plane ticket to get to the meeting. The speaking event you've envisioned (and prepared for) cannot happen without the venue, the PA, the refreshments or the audience members.

When your assistant feels empowered, with the authority to make decisions, you will enjoy more creative solutions for your organization, as well as the freedom that comes with having a trustworthy representative who acts independently, with integrity.

Energize and Encourage your Executive Assistant

An executive assistant should feel empowered to act as a free-thinking, autonomous individual with your best interest in mind. Micromanagement can discourage even the most intelligent, level-headed assistant; whereas empowering that person can lead to the formation of a super-team!

- **Share your goals and your organization's culture with your assistant.** And let the supervision end there. Allow him or her to execute tasks in ways they see fit, and in ways that make them feel comfortable and accomplished.

- **Give your assistant the freedom to be creative, and to make decisions in the

interest of success. The person you've chosen for this position should be someone who shares your values and who respects your vision—and therefore, someone you can trust to find the most efficient and effective way to gain the results you want.

- **Show respect to your assistant in all situations.** Mutual respect should never be dependent on relative social or professional positions.

- **Demonstrate trust in your assistant by sharing low-level confidential information.** Trust is mutual, and is built over time with small demonstrations of honesty and dependability.

- **Set the bar by acting with integrity in all situations—even when your assistant is not present.** He or she sees practically everything, and will set his or her standards for what's expected of them based on what you expect of yourself.

- **Keep the lines of communication open, and avoid being vague or guarded with your wishes.** Only when there is clarity can there be productive interaction and achievement.

- **Empower your assistant with tools that enhance efficiency and productivity.** This will not only benefit the both of you, it will demonstrate your concern for your assistant's well-being and comfort.

- **Protect your assistant from the mundane.** Give him or her special tasks that make them feel like an invaluable team member.

- **Acknowledge your assistant's work, with the understanding that your accomplishments belong to them, too.** Needing to feel appreciated is a basic human need.

"Delegate to Elevate."

—Coach Davenport

Tip #20
Ride Tailwinds, Respect Headwinds

Recognize whether elements are working for you or against you, then make adjustments for best results.

Whether you're the leader of one, ten or thousands, it can seem like the "force" is not always with you. It can feel like you're running into the wind, or fighting against elements that have the power to destroy you.

Here's what often happens: We cruise along happily until something stands in our way or slows our progress. That's when we muster all the assets we have to rail against that hindrance. We fight it. We expend our resources trying to destroy it, get around it, find a way over it...and when we finally feel like we're making some headway, along comes another obstacle.

There is another way, and if you're willing to entertain the idea that it's more effective to Ride Tailwinds and Respect Headwinds, then you'll find yourself fighting less and winning more.

The Power of Appropriate Adjustment

Michael scans his company's first-quarter earnings as the pilot announces the plane will be landing at LaGuardia 30 minutes ahead of schedule. "Wow, no turbulence AND an early arrival," Michael whispers under his breath. "Gotta love a good tailwind."

He turns back to his earnings. Low fuel prices and a grant issued for the purchase of a fuel-efficient fleet have driven his best quarter yet. The new account he just picked up is going to demand a 15% increase in manufacturing. That means more product to deliver...at a profit.

The tailwinds are working for me, he thinks. Better ride this while we can. I'll have Marjorie schedule a meeting with ABC Company tomorrow. Now is the time.

While Michael is speeding toward New York, Lacey is headed west, for LAX. Their flights are the same distance, but hers will be one hour longer, due to headwinds. She reclines her seat and stares out the window over the patchwork quilt of the Midwest. She needs a plan—her beverage company's profits are suffering, due in large part to an upswing in the healthful lifestyles of her once-loyal customers. External forces are slowing her company's progress. She cannot change those forces; however, she can adjust her business's strategy.

That's when she notices a shift in the wing's angle. She feels the plane lift. There's a bump, the flight attendant assures her it's just a bit of turbulence, and Lacey resolves to enjoy the view. It's nothing she hasn't experienced before.

She decides that when she lands, she will seek out a consultant in the health food sector. She has a choice, and she WILL make an adjustment.

Both Michael and Lacey recognized they were experiencing a tailwind and a headwind, respectively, both literally and figuratively. Michael was careful not to squander the opportunity that low fuel costs and a generous grant were affording him, while Lacey resolved to adjust in areas she could control, rather than lament the things that were outside her power.

Both identified forces working for and against them, and took action. Instead of reacting, they chose to respond in a manner that was appropriate, relevant, and proactive.

You can do the same. You can pay close attention to what's going on outside your business, and use the tools within your power to either take advantage of windfalls or to counteract misfortune. These external forces have the potential to affect *everyone* in your market or your league; what will separate the successes from the failures is how each organization responds.

> *"Your astute rate of change is what many call luck."*
>
> —Coach Davenport

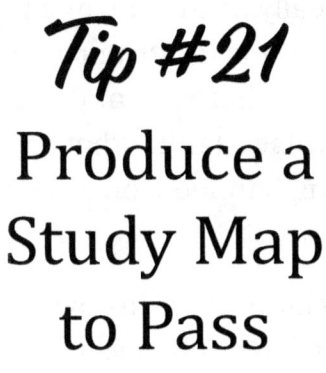

Tip #21
Produce a Study Map to Pass

Where there's commitment to preparation, you can pass with flying colors in a single attempt.

Before you embark on a journey to a destination, you plan your course. You know in which direction you'll turn out of your driveway. You know in which direction you'll be headed, and on which major route(s) you'll be traveling.

This is not a sightseeing tour. It's not a joyride. You must arrive at your destination by a particular time, and you plan on getting there on the first attempt.

And so, you plan ahead.

The same is true if you're in finance, real estate, law... any industry, really...and you must pass an exam in order to work or make advancements in your field. You've got to pass that test, and you'd prefer to do it the first time. In fact, failing that test more than once could mean being banned from doing business in your industry.

The most crucial factor in passing exams is not your test-taking competency. It's not your level of intelligence, or how many cups of coffee you had that morning. Preparation is the key to success—but not just any kind of preparation will do. You're going to need a Study Map.

Chart Your Course with a Study Map

There's a formula for passing crucial exams the first time, every time. It involves creating and following a Study Map that will guide you to gathering all the information you'll need to score well and move forward on your path.

Use this Study Map formula whenever you're facing a test of any type.

- **Create a timeline for your Study Map.** Do this by determining on what date you'll need to pass the exam. Then flip through the required reading material, determine how long it will take you to read it at a leisurely pace, add time for taking 15 practice tests and attending a 3-day class, and then you'll know when you need to start reading.

- **Find someone who's willing to hold you accountable for your exam preparation.** This can be a coach, colleague, relative, friend, boss, mentor...someone who wants to see you succeed and understands the volume of work involved with passing.

- **Read the book, just like you're reading a novel or a newspaper.** Take any practice quizzes at the end of the chapters. Take note of how well you do, but don't take the time to figure out why something is right or wrong; simply move through the book.

- **When you're finished reading the book, take 5 complete practice exams under test conditions.** This means if the final exam will be held at a testing center with a time limit, then you'll want to sit upright in a chair, at a desk or table, in a quiet room, with a timer set just as it will be on test day. Most people score around 40 or 50% the first time around. Take note of the one or two areas where you struggled the most, and go back and re-read those chapters. Take another practice exam. Reread problem areas. Repeat 3 more times, for a total of 5, revisiting no more than the 2 most challenging chapters each time. Your score should improve slightly with each practice test.

- **Attend the class provided to those who will be taking the final exam.** Because you've already read the book and taken 5 practice exams, you will recognize the terms the instructor will use, points will be solidified in your mind because they're not foreign, and you will be more likely to have relevant questions regarding the material.

- **Take 10 more practice exams, texting your score to your mentor after each test.** Be ready for your "Break Out" Score and EXPECT to PASS!

Industry exams are quite difficult, because those industries only want people who can focus and perform under pressure (like time limits). Questions are written using double negatives and a number of answers that may apply, to challenge your critical thinking skills and test your preparedness.

As you follow your Study Map, know that during each stage you should be setting a goal line. Know when you'll finish reading the book, when you'll complete the 5 practice exams, when the class is scheduled, when you'll take the 10 additional practice exams, and when you'll take the final exam.

Follow your Study Map, stay committed, stay focused, don't cut corners…and *not* passing will *not* be a possibility.

> *"Study Maps prepare us to pass the 1st time."*
>
> *—Coach Davenport*

Tip #22
Act Aggressively, with Patience

You have complete control over your commitment to act; you have no control over how the results will come.

What is your intention? And your purpose? When we act in the interest of accomplishment, intention and purpose should be our focus—not the outcome.

This runs counter to the way many of us have been taught to think about the things we want to accomplish. We've been told to envision the precise outcome and to do the work necessary for making it all happen in the way we choose.

But, as you may have found out the hard way, results don't always come when you think they should. They're often packaged differently from how you had envisioned them. And they don't always affect you (and others) in the ways you had anticipated.

Does that mean you didn't accomplish your goal?

Or does it mean you failed when the outcome doesn't look as you believed it should?

Absolutely not! In fact, I think it's safe to say that your control lies in how passionately you do the work, in pursuit of the best possible outcome. It's not your place to concern yourself with how that outcome will look or when it will come.

Take Control Only Over Things Within Your Power

You've heard that good things take time. You may have also heard that you should enjoy the process, rather than always chasing the prize.

But, whether you're in business, sports, family…it can be difficult to wait for the good things you want and deserve—especially when you know exactly what that "should" look like.

But here's the thing you might be missing: Not all good things happen in the timeline you've prepared. For reasons unknown to you, now might not be the best time for that promotion, or for that state championship. Maybe next year is the time...or the next, or the next. Maybe you'll be more prepared then, or maybe the people who really need to see you advance aren't quite ready for you yet.

So instead of asking why, shift your focus.

Instead of directing all your attention to the outcome, why not dive aggressively into the actions you know are necessary for the success you crave?

Act purposefully, with these points in mind:

- **Stop procrastinating.** Take action, no matter how small, today.

- **Avoid distraction.** Focus only on those tasks that will move you toward your objective.

- **Be flexible in the process.** Understand that you may not advance in the exact way you've envisioned. Be ready to make adjustments, as needed.

- **Enjoy the process.** You love what you do, right? That means you should feel rewarded by the work, not just the result. If you don't, you need to find another career or project.

- **Surrender control of the outcome.** When you put in the work, and stay focused and have patience, the outcome is likely to be better than you imagined. If, on the other hand, you remain fixated on a particular result, you will limit your potential.

It's human nature to want to control our environments, or other people, or outside circumstances. Why? Because we think if we can change the exterior forces that are standing in our way, then we can have everything we want.

You will never have complete control over anything outside your own decisions.

So, for the best outcomes in all situations, act aggressively in pursuit of your goals. Allow the process to unfold as it will, to reveal an outcome that is better than you could ever "control" into existence.

"We CAN Recruit ourselves out of any situation, period!"

—Coach Davenport

Tip #23
Name One Word for the Coming Year

You can use words to describe the year that has happened TO you, or you can choose one word that will describe the year that will happen FOR you.

It has been said we cannot control the things that happen to us, but we can control how we react to those things. To take that concept one step further, I'd like to propose that we cannot control what will happen in the coming year, but we can definitely have an influence over it!

It can be easy to find yourself halfway through any given year, saying, "This has not been a good one," or, "I'm finished with this year." The irony of these types of statements is that most of the time, an intention was never set for how that year would feel. A decision about how you would respond to outside stimuli was never made. And so, a year can feel far, far outside your control.

You can change this. You can set your intention for how you will respond, how you will make decisions, how you will view your surroundings and opportunities in the coming year...with one little word.

What word is that?

Let's find out.

One Little Word, One Big Commitment

Brenna and Emily, colleagues in the financial services sector, meet for lunch. It's a busy time, the week between Christmas and the new year, and they both agree they deserve a break.

As they take their seats and wait for their server to arrive, Brenna says, "I just can't believe how bad this year has been." She rubs her temples. "I lost two major clients, the firm downsized so I got demoted, I gained twenty pounds, and my grandma died." She shakes her head. "I think my word for this past year is DISASTER."

Emily extends her hand to her friend. "I'm sorry, Bren. I know it seems bad right now, but just remember that you did pick up some new clients, you still have your job, you look great, and your grandma had a long, wonderful life."

"Ugh, how can you be so positive about everything?"

"The more I appreciate, the more I receive," replies Emily.

"Didn't anything bad happen to you this year? I mean, what word would you use to describe your year?"

"I already decided last January that it would be BLESSED, and so it was."

Ever since the Merriam Webster and Oxford Dictionaries started publishing their Word of the Year, the in-vogue thing has been to talk about years as they happened... to us. This can be a fun way to reflect as a society, but when it comes to YOUR year, do you want to reflect on what has been, or would you rather influence what can be?

Think about your goals. Think about the difference you wish to make, and the influence you want to have. Think about the people who need you most (and what they need from you). Think about what you wish to receive as a result of your work, as well as how you want to feel about the work you do on a daily basis.

And then choose a word that wraps it all up in a nice, neat, descriptive package. Post that word at your desk, on your car's dashboard, on your alarm clock, on your bathroom mirror…so that in all situations throughout the year, you will use that word to guide your decisions.

Follow this formula, and at the end of the year, it will be the only word that fits when describing the past 365 days.

"It was an IM-possible dream, now I'M living it!"

—Coach Davenport

Tip #24
Apply the 24-Hour Rule

Never wait more than 24 hours to respond, but always wait more than 24 hours to react.

There is a distinct difference between responding and reacting. A response is generally thoughtful, appropriate and done with consideration for everyone involved. A reaction, on the other hand, is based on emotion rather than reason, and is often rooted in selfishness and can be a catalyst for further animosity. Reactions aren't always negative, but for the sake of this Tip, we will focus on those reactions that spring from feelings of anger, embarrassment, envy and more.

So when we talk about responding within 24 hours, we're talking about returning phone calls, emails, text messages...because when you are timely in your communications, it speaks volumes about your level of responsibility and attentiveness to the people you work with.

If, however, something throws you into a negative emotion and you're tempted to lash out with a knee-jerk reaction, stop. Wait 24 hours. Do not immediately reply unless it's "I will get back to you about this tomorrow."

How can you tell the difference? And how can you work to control negative reactions that could harm your reputation and your relationships?

It can be as simple as developing an awareness of the differences between responses and reactions.

Responses vs Reactions

You can learn to feel the difference between Responses and Reactions, and use that awareness to apply the 24-Hour Rule. Remember: Responses should be immediate and Reactions should wait until they turn into Responses. This might require some practice to get it right, since your inclination may run counter to the rule.

Response: A product of the thinking brain.
Reaction: A product of the reptilian brain.

Response: A conscious action.
Reaction: A subconscious action.

Response: Takes others' feelings and wellbeing into consideration.
Reaction: Is a selfish act that might hurt others.

Response: The result of careful consideration of the facts.
Reaction: The result of fear or anger.

Response: Builds up relationships.
Reaction: Breaks down relationships.

In addition to all the benefits that responding in a timely (and appropriate) manner offers, there's one more beautiful side effect: When you wait 24 hours, instead of reacting, the fear, anger, envy...or whatever is causing you to want to react, is often overpowered by reason. Those negative emotions subside and you're able to think more clearly and respond in a way that will preserve your character and build respect.

When you're operating as a busy leader of a productive team, it can be tempting to push the mundane to the side and to focus on those things that cause reactions within you.

Work to shift your focus with the 24-Hour Rule. Be the leader who is highly responsive to those communications that may seem mundane, but are actually reputation and integrity builders. And when you feel yourself wanting to lash out, or react, stop and give yourself 24 hours to be the leader you want to be.

"Take Time To Think Today!"
—Coach Davenport

"Leadership always matters."
—Coach Davenport

#1 TEAM!

Tip #25
Experience Role play, with Rules

In the brain, imagination and experience hold the same value.

If you're at all familiar with the Law of Attraction (or The Secret), you know that visioning is important to success. If you're a keynote speaker at an upcoming event, for instance, you should imagine yourself "killin' it"…being witty and fascinating, enthralling the audience, making lasting impressions. Then, you are far more likely to execute your presentation in a fashion worthy of repeat business.

Along those same lines, if you fixate your mind on failure—if you envision yourself stuttering, losing their attention and getting booed out of the room—then, that's what is likely to manifest.

Why is this? How is it possible that we have the power to imagine ourselves into success or failure?

There's the theory that The Universe picks up on your desires and delivers. There's also the science that tells us how brain changes are nearly identical whether we actually experience something, or we imagine or practice experiencing it.

Patients suffering from detrimental illness, or those being physically rehabilitated after an accident, have been shown to recover more quickly when they envision their cells, bones, and muscles healing. The brain even sends out chemical signals that you're full after you imagine eating. It really is that powerful.

How much "experience" could you gain through practice, or Role playing?

You could walk into your very first speaking engagement, test event, sale, or performance as a virtual expert.

Imagine Your Way to Success

There are countless stories and studies that demonstrate the power of practice, imagination and role playing.

There's the story of a prisoner in the USSR who spent nine years in confinement envisioning mental chess games. After being released, he beat the reigning world champion.

Brain scans on weightlifters show that the same areas of the brain light up when they're lifting as when they're thinking about lifting.

A study has shown that people who went to the gym to work out increased muscle mass by 30%, while those who just imagined themselves working out increased their muscle mass by 13.5% (Yue).

Does this mean you can skip the work and just imagine success? Not quite. What it does mean is that you should do both for ultimate results.

When you're learning a new language, preparing for a test, rehearsing a speech, practicing closing a sale, drilling before a game…you can apply these Rules for Role play to enhance your chances of **WINNING BIG:**

- **Simulate the environment in which you will be performing.** If you expect to be onstage with a handheld microphone, then use props to create that scene.

- **Ask friends or colleagues to participate.** They can play the part of the audience, of other test-takers, of the opposing team, or of any characters you need to make the role playing situation seem more authentic.

- **Imagine problems (one at a time) arising.** Decide on the best way to handle the situation, and play that role.

- **Seeing is believing** record yourself, then watch the video, ideally with someone else whom you trust for a well-rounded debrief.

- **Know that it's okay to feel uncomfortable in your role play.** This will mimic the nervousness you might feel the day of the event. Accept it. Work through it. Run through the scenario until your anxiety subsides.

- **When the day of the event rolls around, rely on the experience your brain has accumulated.** It counts, it matters, and it has prepared you.

No one likes walking into a new situation cold, with no idea about what to expect, or how they will perform. By using role play, you can create experiences for your brain to lean on, for confidence *and* accomplishment!

"Create experience before it arrives, and you're already a pro."

—Coach Davenport

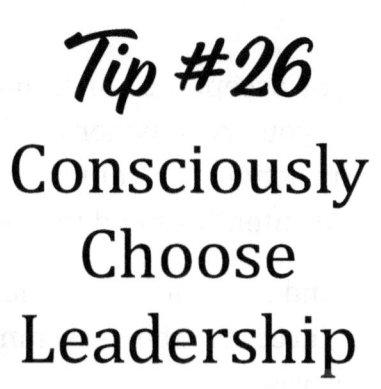

Tip #26
Consciously Choose Leadership

Mothers, Fathers and Leaders resolve to carry a weight—a weight they welcome, accept and fully embody.

Motherhood and Fatherhood are distinct and reputable designations. There are no breaks. There are no freebies. Even when the children are sleeping, or at a friend's house, or off at college…the accountability for being available to those children does not end.

Those children require awareness of the role you've accepted, 24 hours a day, 7 days a week, 365 days a year...even when you're no longer waking up for 2 am feedings.

Similarly, when you accept the honor and responsibility of being a leader, you are a leader at all times. In your thoughts, in your actions, in your availability, in your demeanor, in your intentions and in your choices.

It does not end. And a true leader—one who freely and enthusiastically accepts the assignment—wouldn't have it any other way.

The Weight that a Leader Eagerly Bears

For eight straight years, lifelong friends had gathered in the Outer Banks for a week of rest, relaxation, friendship, and intense partying. The running joke had been that anyone who woke up before noon didn't drink enough the night before.

The group took a few years off. There were marriages, births, careers, student loans...all of which meant limited time and funds for vacation.

But now, the tradition continues. Young parents, exhausted from a long trip, pull up to the familiar beach house in minivans busting with sleeping babies, screaming toddlers and young children trembling with excitement. "When are we going to the ocean?" "Let's pick our bedroom!" "Look at the pool!"

The next morning, following a half-hour boogie-board, umbrella, towel, diaper-bag, child-laden trek to the sand, and then another half-hour spent setting up safe areas for the children...the mothers fall into their beach chairs and the fathers carry the kids down to the water.

"This used to be so much easier," states Tracy. "Remember when all we needed was a cooler and a towel?"

The rest of the women laugh as they count the children in the water with their fathers.

"It's so different now," agrees Beth.

Beth is the only one of the six who has not yet started a family. She's been focused on setting her career in motion, and has just completed her first year as a middle-school principal.

"What are you talking about, Beth?" replies Lisa. "You don't have a worry in the world. If I were you, I'd still be in bed."

"I've grown up, too." Beth rubs sunscreen onto her face. "I'm responsible for the safety and wellbeing of so many children that it's changed the way I live my entire life...even on vacation, 300 miles away from them. It's hard to explain, but I wouldn't have it any other way."

"I know exactly what you're feeling," adds Tracy. "Being responsible for other humans changes your entire outlook."

"But that doesn't mean we're not having wine with dinner!" adds Emily.

"Cheers to that!" they all shout.

Leadership is an extraordinary thing. Before you're ready, it can seem like an impossible task. There are so many things to sacrifice; so many things you're just not willing to give up.

And when it's time to decide to take on the responsibility of being a leader, the job sounds daunting, and you just don't know if you have what is required.

But then you take the leap, because you're drawn to it and you feel that you're being called to something greater. And before you know it, your entire outlook on life transforms. You start to recognize the ripple effects of every decision you make. You become vigilant. Your awareness develops. You begin to feel the weight—and it's the best feeling in the world.

> *"No one said you had to become a leader. No one says you have to stay a leader. But if you choose to be a leader, then always act as a leader. This is an enormous responsibility."*
>
> *—Coach Davenport*

Tip #27
Earn Respect with L.E.A.D.E.R.S.

Be a leader in all aspects, but follow those leaders who have done it right.

Not every leader does it the same way, but all L.E.A.D.E.R.S. have a few things in common.

That's because there's a proven method for what works. Like a tried-and-tested scientific formula, there are facets of leadership forged in the steel of success.

When we look to those who have gone before us, as well as those with promise to continue the legacy, we see the past and present demonstration, or the future potential, to:

Learn

Exercise

Account-Ability

Develop

Expect

Recognize

Set Goals

How many of those actions are you engaging in on an everyday basis? The number of these behaviors that you master will stand in direct correlation to the respect you earn from your team.

L.E.A.D.E.R.S. Earn Respect Like This

Leaders **LEARN**: There's no such thing as a born leader. There are, however, people who are born with an ability to absorb information, and a desire to LEARN how leadership works. These people look to skilled leaders who have gone before them. They study the situational decisions that were made, as well as how those leaders recovered after poor choices and failures. Learning is paramount to effective leadership. Stop learning, and you'll stop leading.

Leaders **EXERCISE**: We all know the difference between talk and action—and we all know where the value lies. Leaders are high-value members of any successful system, and the good ones are known for always putting targeted action ahead of empty words. What's more, the people who rely on them for direction know that when they receive instructions, they can count on that leader to exercise that same advice—to *walk the walk*.

Leaders are **ACCOUNTABLE**: All the things success relies upon are rooted in responsibility. When there's a mistake made, a great leader remains accountable. When something was missed, or someone went unsupported, that same leader takes responsibility for his or her part. And when the entire team experiences a set-back, the leader understands his or her own role in that failure. By demonstrating accountability, a leader sets an example that creates a culture where blame is non-existent and victory is expected.

Leaders **DEVELOP**: A good leader understands that continual development is necessary for growth and expansion. An *exceptional* leader recognizes that development which excludes any level, including the highest honor of leadership, is for naught. There is always room for improvement. There's always something to learn, there are always relationships to nurture, and there's always a higher level to achieve.

Leaders set **EXPECTATIONS**: No great leader believes that all circumstances are immovable; and no great leader accepts the status quo just because that's the way it's always been done. Instead, they raise the bar high and set an example for ruthless go-getting and the thrill that comes from meeting the most challenging of expectations.

Leaders **RECOGNIZE**: The highest-achieving leaders work with their eyes wide open, in order to see and learn what works and what doesn't. And through vigilance, they come to recognize opportunity as well as danger, so they can steer their ship in the direction of the best interest for all involved. Those same leaders also recognize the talent in their team, the evidence of passion and hard work, and they reward those team members for jobs well-done.

Leaders **SET GOALS**: By knowing where they're going, a focused leader multiplies his or her chances of arrival. When no destination is set, arrival is not even a possibility. A skillful leader will set a goal for everything he or she wishes to accomplish—with small goals all along the way.

> *"There is no wrong time to do the RIGHT thing."*
> —Coach Davenport

Tip #28
Recite the Champion's Creed

Today's procrastination guarantees tomorrow's misery.

As a leader, you have a responsibility to act as quickly as possible—not only in situations where time is of the essence, but also in regard to those things you can choose to put off until tomorrow.

Circumstances rarely improve from day-to-day. In fact, most of those circumstances will deteriorate the longer they are allowed to simmer. That means swift action is almost always the best choice. "Nip it in the bud" if you will. "Don't put off until tomorrow what can be done today" if you prefer.

Many leaders experience anxiety about bustin' a move: whether that move is making a decision or starting a project, delivering bad news or trying something new. What's the best advice for those feeling the pressure? Even if your action results in a poor outcome, better for it to happen earlier than later. Think about that: You'll have more time to correct your missteps, more time to gather feedback, more time to spend moving forward rather than standing still.

And that's why the Champion's Creed should be something you recite every day, in the best interest of tomorrow:

> **Make today count so we can take tomorrow off.**

And if you make today count, but decide not to take tomorrow off, because you're preparing to free up the next tomorrow, you'll find yourself astonished at how much you've accomplished after just a few days in this champion mindset.

Conquer Anything with the Champion's Creed

Great leaders have a lot in common with one another. One thing they all do is get things done, without procrastinating.

- When you take time to think about a situation (and what to do about it), make sure you're not really just putting if off until tomorrow because you don't want to do it today. Tomorrow will not change your taste for the decision or the task. In fact, you'll probably be even less eager to do it.

- Any progress beats no progress. Even if you move forward in the wrong direction, it's movement—which is always more productive than stagnation. If you experience a setback, you've gotten it out of the way, and will have learned not to do that again.

- A lack of action can stain your reputation as a leader and instill fear in your team. If the boss is afraid to move forward, everyone else will lose confidence. If the boss lacks incentive, there's nothing inspiring the team to act. Lead by example, to sponsor continual task-blasting.

- Looking back on the time allowed for any decision or task can reflect badly on your leadership role. For instance, if you wait until the day before a lay-off to break the news to your leadership team and they find out you have known for weeks, you will run the risk of losing their respect and worse, their trust. Obviously, if for legal reasons you cannot share anything with anyone, such as a signed NDA, that would take precedence.

- Acting early leaves more time for apologies. As leaders, we must accept responsibility for our actions and avoid blame and finger-pointing in all situations. When you act today, you will have time tomorrow to ask for forgiveness if it didn't work out as planned.

With only a few exceptions, sooner is always better than later when it comes to leadership.

Recite the Champion's Creed, remembering that when we choose to put off until tomorrow what can be conquered today, we decide that every tomorrow will be filled with things we'd rather not do. Make the shift. Do it today. It's time to start looking forward to every tomorrow, rather than spending today dreading it.

"This is how we start Yesterday."

—Coach Davenport

Tip #29
Listen and Be Memorable

Pay attention. Make it yours. Then give them what they need to make it theirs.

When we think about listening, we think about committing the things others say to memory. After all, without being present and paying attention, we can't expect to retain anything they're telling us, right?

But what if I told you that listening is really for an entirely different purpose? What if I told you that listening—and I mean *really* listening—is the foundation of making *yourself* memorable?

You see, listening from a position of leadership is all about gathering information so you can dip into your bag of ideas, take your client (colleague, team or family member) on a journey, add value, provide a solution and walk away memorable.

See how that works? When you listen, you can devise ways to make yourself memorable in that distinct situation, for that specific person or people, for their unique needs. You will walk away from that stage, boardroom, dining room table, court or field as the propagator of an unforgettable message.

How to be Unforgettable

Marianne met with a new client. It was just another typical sales call...his team's passion was wavering; they were no longer striving for excellence. He wondered if they were bored, or maybe feeling under-appreciated. The company's numbers were plummeting and the spark was gone.

Same old story. A manager or business owner no longer knows how to motivate the team, and so they contact ABC Business Consulting to book a speaker who can light a fire in them. Blah, blah, blah. That's all Marianne hears anymore. They all want the same thing.

And so, the following week, she delivers her typical presentation. Teamwork, passion, support, fun... same-old, same-old.

Months pass and the team is again suffering from lack of inspiration and the symptoms of discontent. Marianne's presentation did not hit the mark. Not one team member even remembers what she talked about.

And so, the manager calls XYZ Business Consulting. This time, he notices that the consultant is really listening. Barry is taking notes; reiterating needs to make sure he understands. He asks questions about the team, about the business's history and the manager's hopes for its future.

Barry leaves and spends two weeks creating a presentation that will be unlike anything else. He knows precisely what this company needs to get its groove back, and he's going to present those ideas in a package that is unique not only to XYZ Business Consulting, but unique to the client's culture and challenges.

When the day comes for Barry to speak, the team is engrossed. They nod their heads. Someone is finally acknowledging what they're feeling. They can identify with his visuals, and they are inspired by the stories he tells and the one-of-a-kind language he's using.

He gets it, they say. And they go away with new enthusiasm for their jobs, anxious to take these ideas to others.

In business, coaching and life, being memorable is the key to spreading your message.

Follow this versatile formula for making your message unforgettable:

1. **Prepare**: Do your homework so you're not going in cold. Clear your mind so you have nothing to focus on except what is being said to you.//
2. **Listen**: Focus, absorb, be certain that you understand.
3. **Dip into your Bag**: Your bag of ideas (compiled from your exclusive experiences) is the toolkit from which you will pull methods for communicating with this particular audience.
4. **Tell a Story**: When you communicate with story, you will take your audience (whether that's one person or one thousand people) on a journey unlike any other—one they won't soon forget.
5. **Add Value**: Give them reason to listen to everything you say by maintaining a spirit of giving. Deliver something no one else can.
6. **Provide a Solution**: This makes the interaction worthwhile, and when you solve a problem that others haven't, you won't be forgotten.
7. **Follow Up**: Exercise leadership by staying in touch, monitoring how your message has been put into action, and watching how that message has been creatively repackaged by those who listened to it.

Picture this formula as a sentence with blanks that can be filled in for any purpose. You will successfully convey your message, and make yourself memorable, in every type of situation.

When you listen, you will cause others to listen—and they will remember.

"Whatever you decide to become, own it."

—Coach Davenport

Accountability Wins!

#1

Tip #30
Plant Seeds

Truly vested team members can see the forest for the seeds.

When you walk through a forest for the first time, what's on your mind? Do you think about how it looked before the seeds germinated? Do you think about how those seeds got there, or who (or what) planted them? How ideal conditions had to be, or how much time it took?

Or, do you simply feel the coolness of its shady cover? Hear the breeze weaving through the leaves?

Maybe you don't see, hear or think about any of that. You just move through it.

No matter how much (or how little) you contemplate the landscape around you, one thing is certain: when you have a hand in planting the seeds that grew into the current circumstance, you have a deeper appreciation for what it is today. You can try to imagine the time and work that went into it, but unless you were there, responsible for its taking root, your awareness will be limited.

That's why it's so important to take your team members from start to finish—from seed to forest—rather than dropping them into the center of a complete (or semi-complete) project. It's also imperative that the team revisits the seed concept on a regular basis, so they can remember from where they've come, and from where they need to start every day.

Even more than seeing the forest for the trees, they need to *see the forest for the seeds*.

Take a Close Look at the Seed

At the start of each season, Coach Vince Lombardi said to The Packers, "This is a football."

Those football players were the best-of-the-best. The majority of them had been playing for most of their lives. Many of them had played for Vince in prior seasons.

Of course, they knew what a football looked like.

Some might have believed that this level of instruction was beneath them. Others chose to listen, learn and continue to grow.

What was Coach Lombardi doing by starting every season with the most basic information? He was planting a seed—a seed that each team member could nurture and grow into his own greatness, all of which would come together in team victory. He was also calling their minds to the seed that had been planted in them years ago—when they were learning the basics of the game.

Along with this football seed came some basic care instructions:

- Offense works to keep the ball.
- Special teams work to secure the ball, or go get it.
- Defense works to take it away.
- Everyone, no matter their role, wants the football.

When leadership uses this "plant a seed" with "basic care instructions" approach to coaching, then every other intricacy of competition—in sports, business and elsewhere—makes more sense and is more likely to result in market share.

When leaders plant seeds with their people (their number-one assets) and give them the skills necessary for nurturing the growth of those seeds, everyone touches it, owns it, and wins.

"Management is easy – Coaching is tough – Leadership is Coachable!"

—Coach Davenport

Coach Davenport's Exercise for You and/or Your Team!

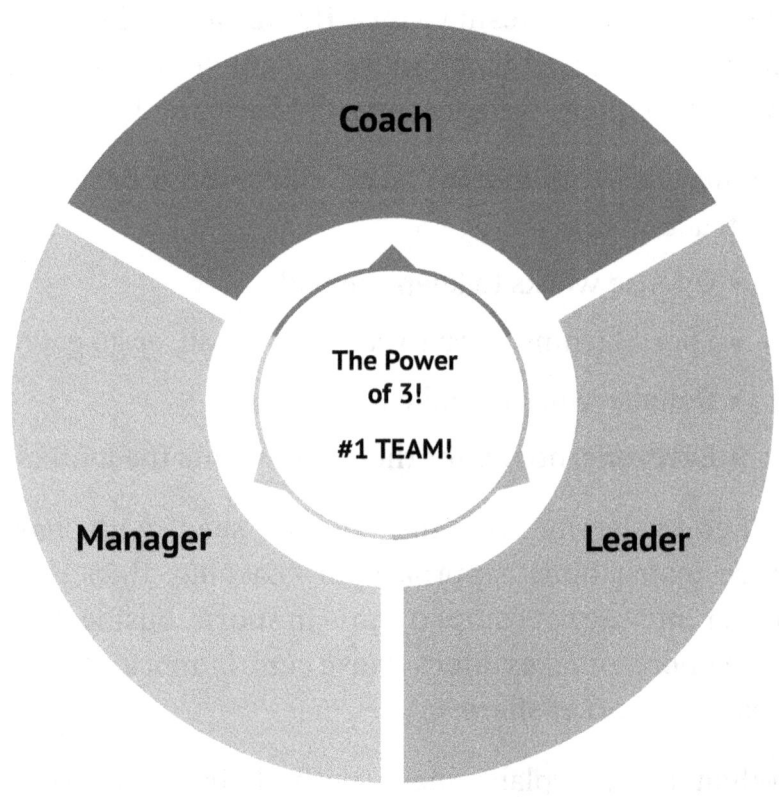

"So goes the leader, so goes the team!"

—Coach Davenport

Please write down one example where YOU have demonstrated the role of each position...

Manager _____
_____
_____

Coach _____
_____
_____

Leader _____
_____
_____

Which role do you believe your greatest strength reside and why?
_____
_____
_____

Which role do you enjoy the most and why?
_____
_____
_____

52 weeks from today which role will you have improved in the most. Why and how?
_____
_____
_____

"Brett has truly been one of the single biggest influences in my career development! His ability to coach actionable skills and then hold me accountable has been a game changer in both my professional and personal life. I feel like Brett is more than a great coach but also a partner and a friend!"

Jim Cotchett, SVP, US Wealth Solutions, Head of Strategic Client Engagement First Eagle Investment Management

"I have been fortunate to see BMD Leadership Institute, Inc up front and in person. I strongly recommend working with them, if you have the opportunity. It will definitely make a big impact in your organization and life."

Darin Miller, Vice President of Operations at Vista Hospitality

"Brett Davenport leads by example. His motivational style encompasses caring, compassion and drive with an energy that allows you to visualize your own success. Brett shows a genuine interest in people and in every one of his projects—he energizes those around him. If you are looking to get to the next level, this is somebody you want to talk to today!"

Kristin Davenport, VP Business Development at Cruise and Vacation Group

"I worked with Brett for the last 7 years of my 30 year career at John Hancock Investments before retiring in May 2019. They were my most productive years in terms of sales, income, and personal growth. I attribute a lot of my success to Brett's coaching. He was fantastic in helping me focus on the day to day tasks/activities that led me to achieve my personal and professional goals."

William McDonough, Realtor at Keller Williams Coastal Lakes & Mountains Realty

"If you are seeking the guidance of a true business and leadership coach, I would highly recommend that you reach out to Brett. Published author, public speaker, trainer and thought-leader, his contribution to businesses and teams are making a huge impact and helping companies in the Syracuse-Auburn area reach their short term goals and find long-term success."

Erika L Davis, CPC, ELI-MP, Certified Professional Coach

"If you want to take your management and leadership skills to the next level or you are looking for a mentor and/or personal and professional "life" coach, Coach Davenport is your man. His passion is contagious and he will challenge you to be your very best. If you bring an open mind and a sincere desire to grow, improve and excel, Coach Davenport will help you achieve your goals. I enjoy working with him."

Ray Hemstreet III, Divisional Vice President

"It is motivating, insightful and fun working with Coach Brett. His thought process is compelling as it clarifies the road map of success. This connection between accountability and achievement is invigorating."

Mark Wiggins, Sales Leader

"Brett has made a positive and decisive impact on my professional and personal life. He is always there consistently helping me generate ideas to improve my business and keep me accountable and I am better for it!"

Matthew Carron, CFP®, CDFA®
Senior Wealth Manager
Heritage Financial

"Brett Davenport came into my life in 1990. In the years since I have come to recognize his unrelenting enthusiasm, his superb interpersonal skills, and his positive personality. He has spent many years learning about, and practicing, the principles he espouses. If you have an opportunity to speak with Brett or read his books, I guarantee you will learn things that will help you, both personally and professionally."

Kevin Hoey Sr., President, HR One Inc.
Senior Vice President- HR One Consulting Inc.

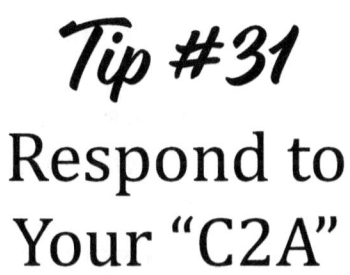

Tip #31
Respond to Your "C2A"

Your title is nothing more than a Call-to-Action.

When you secured your current leadership position, what did the acquisition of that title mean to you? Or when you think of the leadership position you wish to fill someday, what does the prospect of owning that title mean?

Does it mean you'll feel more important? That you'll gain more respect? A higher salary? Notoriety?

Or is your title a Call-to-Action (C2A) that will remind you, every day, of the duty you have to the people you serve?

Here's the truth of the matter: Leadership is Service. The more prestigious the title, the greater your duty to your team. The higher you rise, the greater your C2A.

Leadership is more than a Title

What is a Call-to-Action, anyway? It's typically a term used in marketing; however, it's applicable to life in general. A Call-to-Action is a statement made with the purpose of initiating a specific action. In other words, if you've just introduced your new product on a webpage, and then listed all of its benefits, a Call-to-Action will encourage people to click on a link to buy the product. Or, if you have summarized a problem to your team in a meeting, and asked for their input about possible solutions, your Call-to-Action might be to encourage everyone to submit their feedback the following day.

A Call-to-Action (C2A) should use language that captures attention, encourages participation and inspires people to act.

So with that in mind, what if you were to view your job title as a C2A?

It takes on an entirely new meaning, doesn't it?

> There's a lot of buzz around town about the upcoming primary elections. The borough council has been under serious scrutiny by citizens—and rightly so. The K9 unit has mysteriously lost its private funding. Taxpayer-purchased equipment has been seen on

private property, and official business has been discussed using private emails.

The general consensus, by everyone except the sitting council members, is that it's time for new blood.

Two borough volunteers have been following the chain of events closely. Both want to make a difference, and so they decide to run for borough council.

Daniel, who currently oversees the annual carnival and picnic, has designs on the office of mayor, and sees the council scandal as a way in. He figures that in five years, he can make the connections necessary for raising campaign funds. He closes his eyes and imagines his name on the plaque: 'Daniel McIntown, Mayor'.

Lauren, a volunteer at the Visitor's Center, has also decided to run. She has been speaking with the town's residents, and they've told her they want transparency in spending, and an end to the good-ole-boy/girl culture. They also want Fozzie, the K9 Officer that was forced into retirement, back on patrol. If she were to gain the honor of 'Lauren Landisus, Borough Council', she knows she could make a positive difference. It won't be easy, but she'll work hard because she wants the best for the town (and the people) she loves.

In the primary election, Lauren wins the nomination by a significant margin. Her campaign promises were all about what the people wanted, unlike her opponent's, which were all about his obsession with a future title.

As you move forward with your current title (or toward a future one), avoid wearing it like a badge—like it's something you've earned. Instead, see it as a C2A—something you must work to earn, every day.

> *"You don't need a letter/title to be a leader."*
>
> —Coach Davenport

Tip #32
Maintain Your Message

*Drift in style, drift in delivery...
but let your message be the anchor
that builds trust in your ability.*

When we talk about drift in leadership, we're often referring to the tiny changes in style that occur over time. If you're working with a new team, for a new organization, or under new circumstances, your leadership style might shift in order to accommodate what you need to accomplish...or the people you need to accomplish it with.

This will often happen naturally, as it should, as you maintain a flexible mindset.

Your message, on the other hand, should never change. Remember there are countless ways to deliver a message. You can write a letter, send an email or a text, make a phone call, ask for a meeting, or even send a singing telegram. You might change the way you deliver your message, but never the meaning of it.

Your leadership should be no different.

Pay the Most Mind to the Message

Your message is what you want people to know about you. It's the difference you wish to make and the point you wish to drive home. You will go through different phases of leadership, and each of them will call for you to convey your message in a unique manner.

Should you have the opportunity to reminisce with all the different people you've made contact with in your leadership journey, and if you've done this right, they should all be able to articulate the message you conveyed, no matter how long ago you met them or for how long you worked with them.

What goes into creating this constant, unflappable message? It has to do with a number of things:

- **Your Purpose:** This is your WHY, or the reason you're in a leadership position. It's the thing that drives you to get out of bed every morning, and the thing you picture when you imagine success. It's the people you want to help and the difference you want to make. This should be so branded onto your heart and soul that it will not—it cannot—change.

- **Your Professional Values:** Your professional values are those things you admire in others, and those things you wish to be admired for. They are the positive things that draw you and your people together, and that result in the realization of your purpose. Some examples of professional values are integrity, trustworthiness, fun, accuracy, responsibility, ingenuity, creativity, positive energy and accountablity. The possibilities are endless, only limited by the legacy you wish to leave.

- **Your Passion:** When you find that one thing you love to do above all else—even without being paid—then you have found your passion. Keep working to express this passion, and it will not change. It can be specific or general. It can be tangible or intangible. It's the thing you love most, and when you start to see the fruits of expressing it through your message, it will not fade.

You are the same person today as you were when you first started out. Decades from now, you will be the same person you are today. Sure, you will grow, acquire skills and adjust your leadership style. However, your message should never change, because the person behind that message is, and always has been, YOU.

"Celebrate success, continue to promote the process and always expect to win!"

—Coach Davenport

TOMA™
Top Of Mind Awareness!

#1

Tip #33
Raise Three Process Pillars

A winning process is the foundation of a champion product.

There's a lot of talk about the importance of enjoying the process as much as the product. You've got to love what you do in order to get the best results.

However, there's an element missing from this piece of wisdom. The process that you employ shouldn't simply be enjoyable (although that helps), it should *work*. And in order to find a process that works, you've got to establish a no-fail system that is consistent enough to be functional, and flexible enough to be customizable to any circumstance.

As you move into any mission or project, you can imagine three pillars that support the front of a building. These pillars are load bearing. They are structurally necessary. They are prominent and architecturally sound.

These three pillars should be fundamental to everything you create along your leadership path, and raising them should follow a rehearsed, repeatable procedure. Only with a system such as this can your results be predictable...and triumphant.

The Three Pillars of Process

No matter what type of project you're taking on, or what specific result you're envisioning, you can raise the Three Process Pillars and increase your chances of success.

Here are those pillars:

1. **#1 Challenge:** Name the primary challenge you will face as you move forward. This challenge might be obvious (especially if there is fear involved, or if others have discarded the project because of a particular challenge). Describe this challenge in one or two words and write it in a highly visible spot, to remind yourself on a regular basis what you're working to overcome. You are the protagonist, or main character, in this story. This challenge is the antagonist, or the character trying to block your success. This is something to overcome;

the barrier you must overpower or circumvent in order to move forward, toward victory.

2. **#1 Opportunity:** Every success story has one pivotal opportunity that presented itself (or that was dug up) along the way. This is the opportunity that had the most potential for providing exposure, education, funding, manpower...whatever it is that is most necessary for conquering your #1 Challenge. Without opportunity, the challenge cannot be overcome. Without that challenge, the opportunity would not be fundamental for advancement.

3. **#1 Success:** In order to get the results you want, you must have a vision for what that success will look like. Just as you can't possibly arrive where you're going without knowing where you're headed, you cannot create optimal success without defining what "optimal" looks like before you start. Avoid becoming tied into any specific scenario, but by all means, have an idea of how it will feel and the ripple effects it will create. As you raise this pillar, know where you're going so you can identify the #1 Challenge and the #1 Opportunity for getting there.

As you can see, these Three Process Pillars (#1 Challenge, #1 Opportunity, #1 Success) are not only relied upon for the soundness of the project's structure, they rely upon one another. If you can imagine a magnificent building supported by three pillars, you will start to understand how removing just one of them would cause a problem.

So as you move forward in your leadership role, focus on the Three Process Pillars. Establish a system for getting started on the way to every success. Raise them simultaneously, remembering that omitting a single pillar can result in a weakened, unstable structure. And watch every venture, development and project you build gain in strength and magnificence.

> *"Best 'PRACTICES' lead to successful game days & ultimately championships."*
>
> *—Coach Davenport*

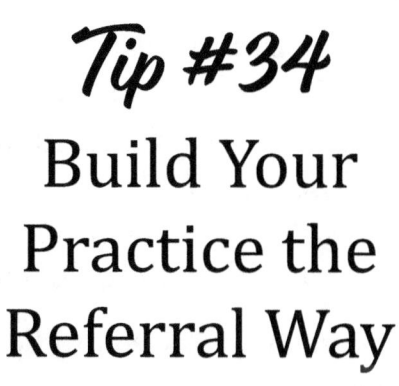

Tip #34
Build Your Practice the Referral Way

When you generate referrals, you are in control of your professional destiny.

In any type of business, referrals are gold. They are the product of word-of-mouth advertising, which costs nothing and yields the highest ROI of any type of marketing.

So instead of waiting for referrals to trickle in, why not create a circumstance in which they flood your business with promise and opportunity?

The Referral Way, Step-by-Step

A. Make an initial call to past colleagues, friends, family and other people you may know.

"Hello <u>THEIR NAME</u>! This is <u>YOUR NAME</u>. Are you still with <u>ABC</u> as a <u>POSITION</u>? We met when I was with <u>XYZ</u>. You may not know that I took an opportunity as a financial advisor with <u>123 FIRM/COMPANY</u>.

I am not calling today to ask you to be my client, like most people would. I am calling for your help! I'd like to ask you three questions. Do you have a few minutes?

Seeing that you're a successful professional, I suspect you already have an advisor, so with that in mind…

1. What is one thing you like most about your advisor?
2. What is one thing you don't like about your advisor?
3. If you had one wish, what would you want your advisor to do more of for you?

<u>THEIR NAME</u>, thank you for your time!"

*** Confirm their BUSINESS address, unless you don't have it, (then ask for it). Keep it business-related, and YES, mail the note in the next step to their place of business. Why? If you receive junk mail every day, like me, you don't open it at *home*, DO YOU?***

B. Send a hand-written thank you note.

THEIR NAME , it was great to hear your voice again! (*this next part should be customized, based on your conversation*) I'm happy to hear of your continued success. Thank you for your time and for answering my three questions! All the best to you!

ENCLOSE YOUR BUSINESS CARD

*** *BE SURE TO USE EXCLAMATION POINT!!!* **Need Enthusiasm!** ***

C. Call back 90-120 days later.

THEIR NAME, it was great speaking with you a few months ago. Our conversation was extremely valuable! In-fact it was so helpful, I'd like to ask you one more question.

My business has been growing and I'm very happy I made the transition! Who is the one person you would recommend I contact to help them with _____?" (*whatever they named as their 'one wish' when you asked question #3*)

THEIR NAME, thank you for your time!"

D. Send another hand-written thank-you note to the Referrer.

THEIR NAME, thank you again for your time and introducing me to NAME OF REFERRAL! The next time you have a conversation with someone who is frustrated with their current advisor, or who is looking for an advisor, please hand them my card! Enjoy your _____! *(fill in the blank...summer, fall, holiday, vacation, etc.)*

I appreciate ALL your help!

ENCLOSE TWO BUSINESS CARDS

E. Call the referral.
"Hello, <u>NAME OF REFERRAL</u>, this is <u>YOUR NAME</u>. We have a mutual friend, <u>REFERRER'S NAME</u>! <u>REFERRER'S NAME</u> and I *(worked together @ EFG Corporation, or are both Members @ 567 Country Club, or both went to NYU, etc.)* and your name came up! I'm confident you already have an advisor who *(manages your investments, etc.)* and that's a good thing! <u>NAME OF REFERRAL</u>, the reason for my call today is to ask for your help! I'd like to ask you three questions! Do you have a couple minutes?

1. What is one thing you like most about your advisor?

2. What is one thing you don't like about your advisor?

3. If you had one wish, what would you want your advisor to do more of for you?

<u>NAME OF REFERRAL</u>, thank you for your time!"

*** Confirm their BUSINESS address, unless you don't have it, (then ask for it). Keep it business-related, and YES, mail the note in the next step to their place of business. Why? If you receive junk mail every day, like me, you don't open it at *home*, DO YOU?***

F. Send a hand-written thank-you note to the referral.
NAME OF REFERRAL, I'm sure glad NAME OF REFERRER introduced us! I enjoyed our conversation! *(this next part should be customized, based on your conversation)* *(your passion when you speak about your family is so inspiring, etc.)* Thank you for your time and for answering my three questions. All the best to you!

ENCLOSE YOUR BUSINESS CARD

*** BE SURE TO USE EXCLAMATION POINT!!! **Need Enthusiasm! *****

G. Call back the referral 90-120 days later.
"NAME OF REFERRAL, it was great speaking with you a few months ago. Our conversation was extremely valuable! In-fact it was so helpful, I'd like to ask you one more question.

My business has been growing and I'm very happy I made the transition! Who is the one person you would recommend I contact to help them with_____?" *(whatever they named as their 'one wish' when you asked question #3)*

NAME OF REFERRAL, thank you for your time!"

H. Send a hand-written thank-you note to the initial Referrer.
NAME of *INITIAL* REFERRER, thank you again for your time and introducing me to NAME OF THEIR REFERRAL! The next time you have a conversation with someone who is frustrated with their current advisor,

or who is looking for an advisor, please hand them my card! Enjoy your ! *(fill in the blank...summer, fall, holiday, vacation, etc.)*

I appreciate ALL your help!

ENCLOSE TWO BUSINESS CARDS

PLEASE make sure everything is LOGGED, put into your CRM...plus track the answers to your three questions to uncover the most common themes and learn from them! This will be your **COMPETITIVE ADVANTAGE!**

REPEAT THE PROCESS, OVER and OVER and OVER. *Make it YOURS!*

GOALS:

___ calls per day

___ thank-you notes per day

___ ?

Remember, that is at least <u>NUMBER</u> calls EVERY DAY you suit up, and then ONE more before you leave, 100% of the time!

All the best, and EXPECT TO WIN!

"If you have a RICH Pipeline, then COI & Referrals will convert it to a WEALTHY one!"

—Coach Davenport

Coach Davenport's Concept of his "Freedom to Win Funnel"

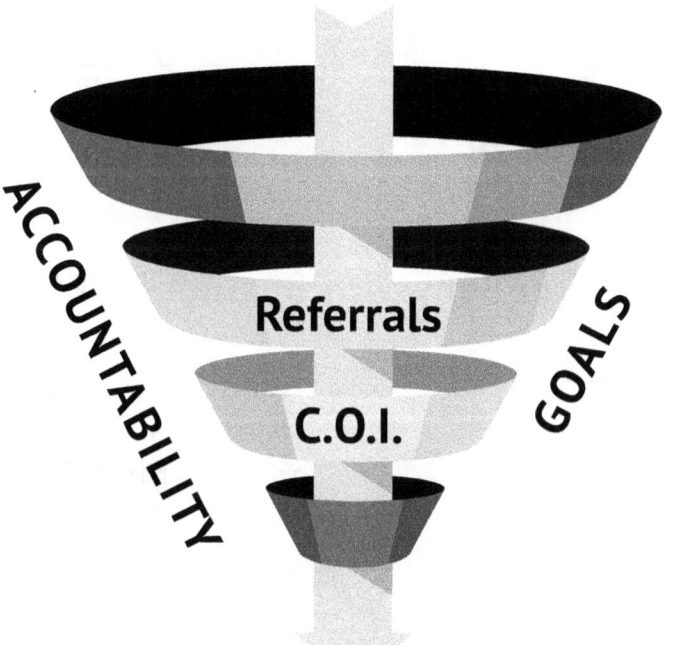

Minimum 4 new names in the pipeline per month!

Before: Captive to Business = Busy

Out of control

Losing

Frustration

No time

Messy

Tired

What 3 "out of balance" feelings would you add to this typical list?

_____

_____

_____

After: Freedom with Business = Efficient

In control

Winning

Gratification

Balance

Clean

Energizing

What 3 "in balance" feelings would you add to this "A" typical list?

_____

_____

_____

"If we are all exhausted, why isn't anything getting done..."

—Coach Davenport

"I have worked with and known Brett for 29 years. He is the ultimate professional and has a unique ability to identify broken sales processes and put an action plan in place that focuses on activity and accountability. He is a great mentor to me and any organization would benefit from his coaching and mentoring skills."

Joe Wetmore, CEO, President, & Co-Founder
ClearBridge Technology Group

"I've had the privilege of knowing Brett for a few decades. He was an incredible mentor to me when I started out in my Finacial Services career. His incredible leadership and determination made such an impact on my life. His positive attitude and winning mentality shaped me to what I am today. I thank you for making such a great impression on me from the day we met. I will always be grateful."

Mark Perry, CMFC, CLTC, CEO, President at Independent Insurance Brokerage, LLC

"In working with me at John Hancock, Brett Davenport, AKA "Coach", has been an incredible source of knowledge and insight to help me grow more in my leadership abilities. In my 12 months with Coach, he has taught me several important lessons that will further guide me as we navigate some upcoming important changes in the future. He is an outstanding executive coach, author, and leader and I would highly recommend him to anyone. Thank you for all that you've done so far Coach!"

Chris Porter, CFP®, CRPS®, Internal Sales Director

"Brett "Coach" Davenport has had a career centered around Leading individuals, teams and organizations to the TOP! Coach Davenport has the unique ability to build successful foundations with anyone, based on experiencing Goal Attainment through his proven practical process of effective Goal Setting! He will challenge you and your team to be their very best through consistent and sustainable accountability on what matters most both personally and professionally! Finally, if you have the opportunity to hear him speak or better yet become your Coach, take it!"

Bill Cates, Client Acquisition Expert

"Brett Davenport has been an integral aspect of my professional development. Not only has he been a guiding force in my own personal achievements, but he has given me the tools and resources to succeed in the business world. Brett's willingness to help the eager individuals that serve him is a true testament to his knowledge of what it takes to build a leader and the secret to surrounding yourself with other successful, driven professionals. He is one of the most inspirational people in the business world today. Be sure to listen when he takes the time to give you advice and encouragement, it will make the difference! Believe."

Ashley Hoey, Senior Manager Awareness and Promotion at Deloitte

Tip #35
Put Me in COACH

Leadership is a contact sport.

"Put me in coach!"

It's what everybody on the bench is thinking. It's our default state of mind when we're in the role of follower. We wait to be acknowledged, and when we are, we run in and tackle someone, or receive a pass, work alongside a co-worker on a project, console someone, share a meal, or start a conversation.

And then, when we're promoted to a leadership position, we adopt a hands-off mentality, like being a leader means we're no longer part of the team—that our days of "getting in there" are over.

Nothing *should* be farther from the truth.

Leadership is a Hands-On Profession

When you get in there as a hands-on leader, you never fully separate yourself from operations. This doesn't mean you should micro-manage or breathe down your team members' necks. What it does mean is that you remain fully accessible, approachable and willing to dig in and get things done as a unit.

An ivory-tower leader, or one who views operations from a distance, will never gain the full respect of his or her team. There's no opportunity for relationship, no proof of passion...no connection.

So what's the right way to roll your sleeves up and jump in? You've got to be there in your head and heart, then all else will follow.

- **Know the mindset of your team.** What are they hoping to achieve? What are their challenges? What makes them feel excited, fulfilled, accomplished? Embody the mindset of your team, and they will see evidence of your interest in every interaction.

- **Know how to do every team member's job.** This is two-fold. Not only will you gain a better understanding of what's involved in day-to-day operations, you will earn the respect of your team members—because when they talk about their problems and achievements, you will have the ability to empathize with them. This doesn't mean you have to be skilled at every position, ready to take over. It simply means you must have an idea of what's required and how difficult it can be to achieve success from any post.

- **Poke your head in.** Never underestimate the power of the periodic check-in. How's it going? Anything you want to talk about? How are you? Questions like this, and attention to the answers, let your team members know that you care and that you're "in there" with them.

- **Take control of the wheel, not the remote.** When change is about to happen, get in the trenches. Keep everyone informed. Be generous with information, welcome questions and answer them honestly. In times of uncertainty, no one wants to look up and see a detached leader pushing buttons and pulling cords. They want to know that you're right there beside them, experiencing the same things they are—and taking charge *on the field*.

- **Fully experience your team.** Leaders never truly realize what a spectacular team they have until they get to know them as a group, and as individuals. Experience your team at eye level. Appreciate just how awesome they are.

Know your operation. Know your team. At all times, be ready to snap into action and be the one they can lean on (literally and figuratively).

Talk is cheap, and it's the equivalent of locking yourself in that ivory tower. Come down to play. Interact and lead from the field.

> *"Time to stop wishing and start working to be the best you can ultimately BE-come."*
>
> —Coach Davenport

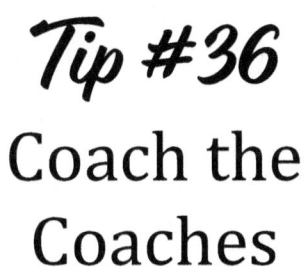

Tip #36
Coach the Coaches

Create your dynasty with a succession of assistant coaches.

How do coaches learn to lead?

Do they wake up one day and take charge? Or do they struggle and stumble along the way, hoping to make the right decisions and minimize failures? Do they pray? Or wish on stars?

The best, most promising coaches look to other leaders for guidance. Talented, driven up-and-coming coaches understand they have a lot to learn and look to successful coaches for advice. They want to be the best they can be, and know that in order to make that happen, they've got to be willing to learn, and they've got to allow themselves to be led.

Every successful leader was once a follower. The distinction between future leaders and those who will forever follow is drive—and a passion to make a unique difference in their family, their workplace, their neighborhood or the world.

Will you be the kind of coach who leads those who want to learn? Will you dip into your bag of tools and impart your ideas to them? So they can lead in a style that supports your legacy?

Passing along what you know about leadership—even if that's limited at this point—is the key to establishing a legacy for yourself. And you can start, today, in the smallest of ways.

Pass it On

As you move through your coaching career, you will come across emerging leaders who are in it for all the wrong reasons. Maybe they're in pursuit of money or notoriety. Maybe they believe that just because they have a loud personality (and an even louder mouth), that they're destined to be in charge. The issue is the role will be all about them, carrying a selfish attitude.

We all know these are typically the wrong choice for leadership, and your assignment as a legacy coach is to prepare your team for this type of individual.

To the contrary, when your path intersects with individuals who have a natural magnetism and charisma—those who gain others' respect the right way and who want to be leaders in order to cause the greatest positive change for all involved—then you have a duty to nurture that leadership seed.

Here are a few guideposts you can refer to as you begin to cultivate the leadership qualities you see in others:

- **Point the spotlight outward.** If you've ever been onstage, you know that the spotlight is blinding. Often, you can't see ten feet in front of you. This is no way to lead (at least on a regular basis). Get behind that spotlight once in a while. Shine it on those who deserve to be seen and heard. The first thing you'll notice is how far and wide your view becomes.

- **Be secure in your position.** Too many coaches fear supporting other coaches—they worry about competition, or that their own shine will be tarnished. Set these feelings aside. Know that the most righteous leaders are those who show other leaders the path to success.

- **Believe in your legacy.** What will live longer? You or the ideas you generate? Long after we're all gone, our messages can live on through the work of others. The only way to make this happen is to touch the lives of other significant influencers.

- **Be willing to follow.** There will always be a coach or leader more experienced or wiser than you. Look to them. Assume the role of follower. Learn and use what they teach you to increase the depth of your knowledge...so you can pass that on to the next generation.

No leader is at the front of the pack at every moment. In fact, you will find that at the most crucial learning points of your career, you will look to others for direction. Practice being the one who not only welcomes that guidance, but who provides it to others who want to learn.

You are a cog in the coaching machine, a link in a leadership legacy. Hold your shape. Receive energy and pass it on.

"Success to Significance is approaching as we advance our Leaders."

—Coach Davenport

Tip #37
Communicate with Purpose

You are in control of the responses you get.

Have you ever felt like no one is listening? Or that no one is understanding what you're trying to say? Do you feel ignored? Or like you're consistently misunderstood?

In any social or professional situation, it's important to isolate ongoing problems and ask yourself *Who or What is the Common Denominator?*

If communication problems are ongoing, then the answer is YOU.

There's one foolproof way to know if your communication skills are adequate: Ask yourself if you're getting the responses you want. Are you closing sales? Are you successfully getting referrals? Are you making connections? Are you building relationships? Are you making a difference?

If you're not getting what you want, it's time to change the ways in which you're asking.

Effective Communication, for Beneficial Connections

Productive communication ends with all parties feeling they've been heard, understood and that they've not only given value, but that they've received value.

The world's most effective and communicative leaders have some things in common. You can learn from them by striving to…

- **Stay Present:** While others are speaking, do not interrupt with your own stories, ask for clarification of details, do not steer the conversation away from the speaker, or allow your mind to wander. Instead, permit others to fully express themselves, and then make observations based on the feelings of the other person, rather than immediately giving advice or solving problems. Ask additional questions.

- **Adjust Style:** Not everyone communicates in the same manner. Some are dominant. Some focus on having influence. Some are compliant. Others are conscientious. Some individuals might thrive on quick delivery with short sentences. Others need to take their time and absorb information. A big part of communicating effectively is determining how people wish to receive material, and then adjust to that so you can make quality connections.

- **Have Empathy:** If you want to make connections, you'll have to learn to put yourself in others' shoes and feel what they're feeling. They will know you've done this when you express genuine compassion and understanding for their circumstances.

- **Go Behind the Words:** When others express themselves with defensiveness or hatred, do not take those words at face value. Instead, look behind the words for the pain, fear or doubt...and have compassion for that.

- **Use your Voice:** Never put your own truth to the side for the sake of peace or to avoid arguments. Instead, speak your truth compassionately, letting others know how you feel, not how they *should* feel. Speak from personal experience, making it clear that your own perceptions are driving you, rather than insisting others agree with you.

- **Look for Common Ground:** There's a saying that it's more important to move forward than it is to always be right. This is true in every form of communication. When we use arguments to communicate, we are generally trying to prove that we're right—and every time this is the focus, nothing gets solved. Instead, take a step back, look at the entire situation from a number of viewpoints, and come to an agreement that benefits everyone involved.

Great communication starts with listening, and it ends with telling your own personal truth. It does not leave you responsible for others' feelings, but it does make you responsible for your own words and actions. It demands that you add value, and that you strive to feel and see what others are perceiving.

When you communicate effectively, there is no agreement outside the realm of possibility. There is no result you cannot achieve.

"It doesn't matter how crystal clear you can hear, if you don't LISTEN..."

—Coach Davenport

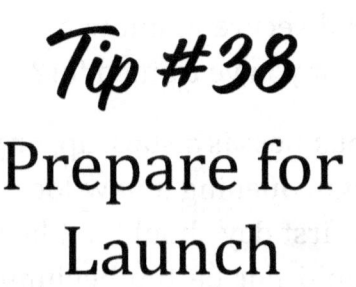

Tip #38
Prepare for Launch

Fill your tank and commission your crew before takeoff.

When you prepare for launch, what comes to mind as the countdown ensues?

3...2...1...

Is that when you start to assign crew members' positions and delegate tasks? Is that when you make sure you have enough fuel and learn to read the gauges? Will you educate yourself on how to fly that craft while you're hurtling through space?

Or will you sit back and watch as the plan you designed plays out in real time? Will you be confident in your preparation and secure in knowing all that's left to do is carry out what you've trained for?

Whether the business is a start-up, or you're launching a new campaign, opening a new location, or leading a new team, the first day should not be your first day on the job. It should not be the beginning of starting to think about strategy, delegation, expectations…in fact, it should be the end of that and the beginning of moving forward with all of that preparation under your belt.

The end of your launch plan is the beginning of the launch.

Before the Launch Comes the Launch Plan

Which comes first? The launch or the plan? This is no chicken-or-egg question. It's far simpler than that.

Too often, opening the doors to the public feels like a beginning, when in fact, it should feel more like the end. The end to the preparation, the tool-gathering and the development. The end to organizing. The end to thinking…and the beginning of doing.

Without all that pre-planning, you might find yourself floundering.

In order to make your launch as smooth (and successful) as possible, employ the OPERATE launch strategy:

O.P.E.R.A.T.E. stands for OWN, PLAN, EXPECT, REHEARSE, AIM, TALK, and EQUIP.

That's the plan; in that order—all before the day of the launch.

- **Own:** Know the purpose of this launch inside and out. Embody it, believe in it, own it. If you don't (or you can't), look at it from a new angle or get a new purpose.

- **Plan:** Put the strategy for the launch in writing. Plan your moves as if you're headed into uncharted territory, because you are.

- **Expect:** Envision what you expect to happen, then create at least three more scenarios. Be prepared for anything.

- **Rehearse:** Imagine how you and your team will roll out the launch, and then practice how you will respond to a variety of circumstances. Then rehearse it again. And again.

- **Aim:** Now that you're rehearsed, your goal is within reach. Set your sights on that goal and narrow your field of vision so you're hyper-focused on it.

- **Talk:** Gather the team and listen to their concerns. Talk about what everyone is expecting, anticipating, fearing…and discuss how the team will handle any of the scenarios that come up.

- **Equip:** Ensure that every team member feels properly equipped for launch, covering situations they may feel uneasy about. Provide the tangible tools they'll need, as well as intangible ones, like mentorship.

Your launch is not a test flight. Ask any seasoned pilot or astronaut and they'll tell you—the day of the launch is simply a replication of all the preparations they've made. If the OPERATE launch plan was carried out correctly, the launch feels like a relief. It feels like the fruit of their labor. It goes smoothly, without a hitch, because they were fully prepared, adequately equipped and well-rehearsed.

"Know what you're not, so you can live who you are to the fullest!"

—*Coach Davenport*

"MAJOR in the MAJORS TODAY with PURPOSE"

–Coach Davenport

#1

Coach Davenport's Exercise for You and/or Your Team!

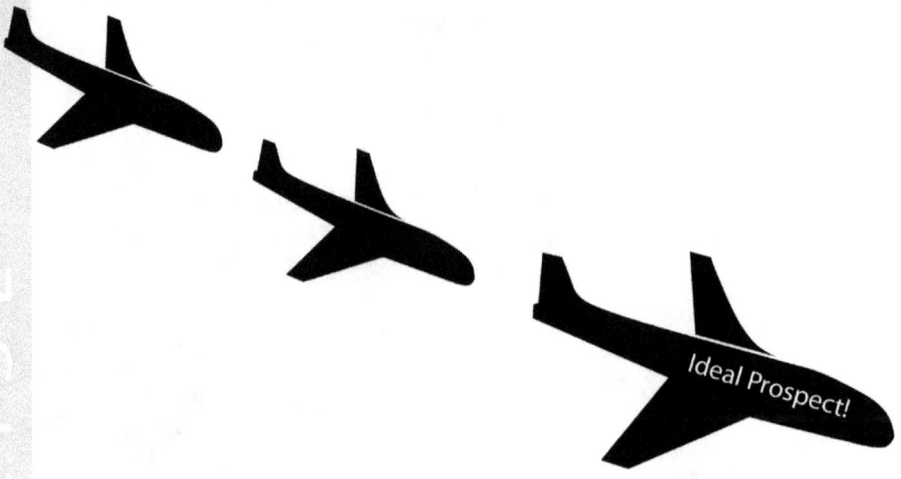

Your Pipeline

1. What is your minimum number of ideal prospects that will land in your pipeline each month? _____

2. How many days does an average ideal prospect reside within your pipeline before they convert to an ideal client? _____

3. What is your closing percentage? _____
   - <u>Critical inspection required</u> if you expect to excel in the personal and professional balanced air space.

Coach Davenport's Exercise for You and/or Your Team!

Your Pipeline

4. How often do you review your pipeline with your team? _____

5. How often will you cleanse your pipeline? _____

6. Finally, please describe "in detail" your ideal client profile!

   _____
   _____
   _____
   _____

"I have used several coaches over the past 36 years, and Coach Brett is by far the best. Setting goals is one thing, but having to be accountable to Brett and laser focused month to month has been a game changer for me. The sales pipeline system we developed has allowed me to track all of my activity and made it easier to update Brett every month on my progress. I am grateful to have him as a coach but also to have him as a friend. I look forward to many years of working with him and crushing my goals.

See you at the top!"

Brad LeBlanc, President of BHL Financial Services

"Through circles of excellence including collaborative business meetings, conferences, and masterminds, I have had the opportunity to witness Brett at his best which is business consulting. If you want to succeed in your business or take your business to a higher level of success, then you will want to invest in his coaching and consulting programs. His clear focus and dedication to great leadership surpasses that of others. Allow him to lead you in the right direction you desire—to the top!"

Dr. Andrea Adams-Miller, MCNLP, MCHT, CNP, NBP, International Publicist & Professional Polymath Implementing Action to Help High-Level Visionaries Achieve Dreams Higher Than They Ever Dared to Desire

"Brett has been my personal business coach for the last 6 yrs. From helping me direct my sales team attain its goals to assistance managing work-life balance, Brett has been outstanding. If you are looking to take the next step in your career or want to revitalize your approach Brett's your guy. I've been in institutional sales and management for over 30 years now. Yes there are new tricks and no this isn't fluff or spin."

Steve Davis, Divisional VP

"I worked closely with "Coach" Brett for over a year...He transformed my professional life and made me realize how to think more clearly about what is most important. His dedication, commitment, expertise, and guidance is unmatched in the industry. He comes prepared and understands the variables needed for someone to excel in this industry. I highly recommend Brett."

Paul Andrulli, CIMA®, SVP, Sales Business Development Manager at First Eagle Investment Management

"Coach Brett has been a godsend helping me through my darkest hour. He helped me get my mind right, regain my confidence, and focus on the positives. I so appreciate and value his advice and wisdom in helping me rebuild my business and confidence. He's a great listener, great motivator, and he's there when you need him. So much to learn from him and blessed to have him in my corner!"

James S. Lin, MBA, CRPC, CPFA, Senior Vice President Financial Advisor, RBC Wealth Management

"I worked with Brett Davenport for over a year and found his coaching and leadership processes extremely helpful in my journey to improve my business and personal life. He is focused, timely, considerate, motivating and especially inspirational. I would highly recommend Brett to anyone finding it difficult to achieve personal and professional goals. He will ensure you are on the right track and most importantly, hold you accountable to what you commit to. Thank you Coach for your leadership. As a result, I EXPECT TO WIN!"

David B. Bonkowski, Principal—Branch Team Market Optimization at Edward Jones

"An Impactful Partnership" is how I would describe my relationship with Coach D! With all of the noise and distractions in today's world and the resulting complexities that come into my business and personal life, Brett's coaching has helped me identify, stay focused, and execute on the specific tasks which lead to professional success and personal fulfilment. I am grateful for both our professional relationship, as well as our friendship."

Bob McDermott, Managing Director, National Sales Manager Insperex

"Before I started working with Coach, my interview skills were mediocre at best. After just 5 sessions, he helped me receive multiple offers and land my first job, I can't thank him enough!"

Tim Dannemann, Management Student at The University of Kentucky

Tip #39
Slow Down to Speed Up

Efficiency is multiplied when the process is scrutinized.

When we think about efficiency, all too often, our minds turn to speed. How fast can you get it done?

And in our haste to reach a conclusion, we tend to overlook quality and learning.

What do I mean by that?

Imagine you and your team find yourself in a dire situation. A contract is about to be lost. Production is down. Or new clients are rolling in, and you must find a way to serve them all. In these scenarios, the temptation might be to slap a Band Aid on the problem; to triage and treat the most damaging symptom; to get out of the most immediate danger in the quickest way possible.

But what is that teaching the team? And how is that ensuring future excellence?

The times when speed seems to be of the essence are the times when slowing down is the most critical.

You've got to slow down in order to speed up.

Eliminate the Fix-it-Fast Culture

Larry and Sean's teams both work in the customer service industry. Larry has a "wing it" attitude about leading his team. "Prepare them, and they can respond to anything" is his team-training motto. "Speed of resolution is the key to success."

Sounds great. Sounds responsive. Sounds efficient. Right?

The only problem? There is no learning experience, no establishment of strategy. The focus is on "Shut them up and get them off the phone as quickly as possible."

Sean's team, on the other hand, has been taught to identify potential customer service issues by stopping, slowing the roll, and asking a series of questions:

- *What is it you're not satisfied with?*

- *How does it differ from what you expected?*
- *What do you see as a reasonable solution?*

And all of these questions should naturally lead to a conversation that not only calms the customer, but resolves the issue and KEEPS the customer. Moreover, it will serve as a learning experience for future, similar situations.

This Slow Down to Speed Up way of thinking is common in sports coaching, too. If the runner is fast, the tendency is to hurry…and that's when errors happen. However, if the fielder slows down, focuses on mechanics, and does their job with deliberation and purpose, the outcome is almost always better than if he would have hurried.

When you Slow Down to Speed Up, you will achieve your objectives more quickly. I know that sounds counterintuitive; however, you're more likely to get it right the first time, and you're more likely to maintain your good reputation for high quality.

It's an exercise in pacing, really—and it takes discipline and practice. In general, when a situation seems dire, and you're tempted to rush through, that's often when slowing down is the most critical. There is always a solution; you simply have to uncover it with probing dialogue, intense focus, and a genuine understanding of the root of the problem.

So lift your foot from the gas pedal a bit, cruise at a controlled rate…and anticipate accelerating at *precisely* the right time.

"Elite Professionals never take a play off, yet they take plenty of time off."

—Coach Davenport

Tip #40
Replace Stubborn with S.M.A.R.T.

S.M.A.R.T. leaders see no reason to resist change.

One of the most poisonous statements to success is "This is the way we've always done it." Let's face it: the world around us is constantly changing, and if we stand firm, stubbornly refusing to adapt, we will be left behind.

It doesn't matter if fear or stubbornness is causing you to resist change; the outcome will be the same. Of course, there's the argument that change isn't always good—that sometimes, the tried-and-tested way is the best way. However, you can't deny that even if the change at hand is considered to be harmful to your organization, you're going to need a strategy for navigating the ripples of that revolution.

So are you going to be stubborn, clinging with white knuckles to the way you've always done it? Or are you going to make the most of every circumstance with a S.M.A.R.T. strategy?

The S.M.A.R.T. Way is the Best Way

Leading your team in the adaptation to change isn't about following all the latest trends or copying your competitors. Instead, it's about staying true to your values, mission, vision, purpose…and uncovering what they look like in action, under a new circumstance.

One way to make sure you're evolving toward growth, as well as honoring your team's values, is to adhere to the S.M.A.R.T. Strategy.

Any time you feel yourself standing stubborn against change, or resisting doing something differently than you have in the past, take yourself through these five steps. Avoid sharing your thought process with your team just yet—you must first get your S.M.A.R.T. Strategy in order.

- **Shift:** First, you've got to shift your mind from a closed to an open state. Be willing to see any circumstance from the viewpoint of your customers, your team members, your competitors, your investors…anyone who could potentially be influenced by the change that's at hand. This doesn't mean you have to compromise your standards; it's simply an exercise in seeing the challenge from all directions, in search of the action (or non-action) that's best for all involved.

- **Maintain:** This is your only chance in this process to be stubborn, so take full advantage of it. Think about your corporate values. What are the ethics you've committed to as a leader of this organization? If everything around you and your team changed, what principles would still need to be intact in order for you to keep the promises you've made? What things need to stay the same in order for you to maintain the reputation you've built? These are your non-negotiables.

- **Assess:** Now it's time to put that new open state of mind and unshakable values to work together. Ask yourself how you can adapt to the change at hand without compromising your values. Also look for how you might enhance the expression of those values in new scenarios. There's a tendency to think that change will always negatively impact your organizations' principles. In many cases, the exact opposite is true, so look for opportunities for development.

- **Reinvent:** Now that you're more comfortable with the concept of change, it's time to rethink the way you will proceed. The way you've always done it isn't always the best way. The willingness to evolve is often far more valuable.

Focus on growth and improvement, remaining stubborn only in regard to your values.

- **Track:** As you proceed, you're going to need to determine whether or not your new approach is working in favor of all involved. This is the time to bring the team in, to advise them of any new approaches and procedures, and to oversee the entire process like the competent leader you're becoming. Keep track of the numbers; gather evidence; invite feedback; take notes. This doesn't have to be an all-or-nothing proposition; maybe some elements of the new approach will work seamlessly, while others need adjustment. Learn as you go. Stay pliable and evolve.

The S.M.A.R.T. Strategy will prove to your team and your organization that you're a leader interested in long-term success, and you will feel the shift the moment you take that first step.

Change brings with it new, exciting opportunities, and when you start to see the potential in that, you will also start to see the potential in yourself.

"The change of habits are to small to notice until they are to strong to be broken."

—Coach Davenport

TEAMWORK!

#1

Coach Davenport's Exercise for You and/or Your Team!

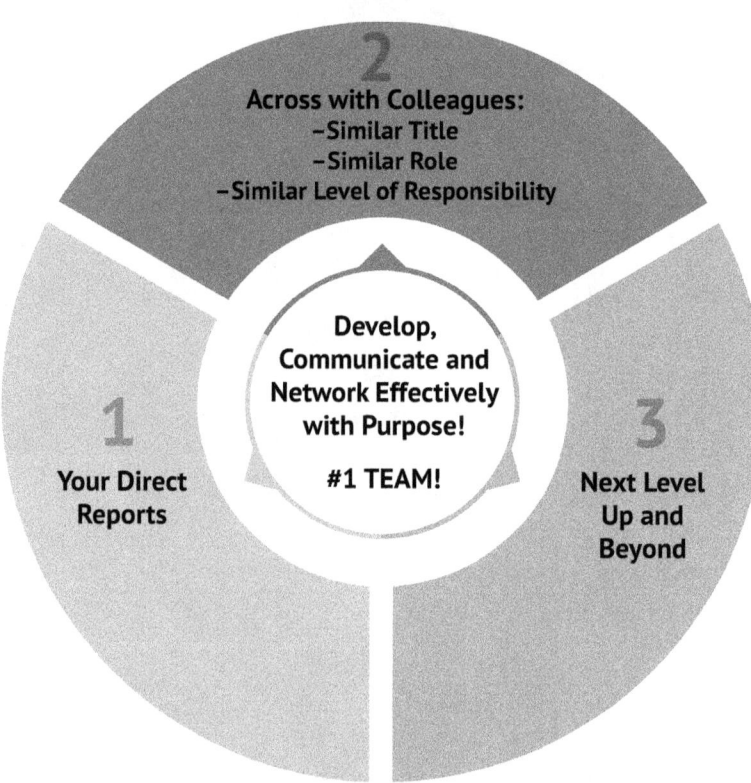

"Inspect what you Expect of your Skill Development."

—Coach Davenport

Replace Stubborn with S.M.A.R.T. | 213

One of the fastest and most difficult ways to advance your career is to be Elite in each of these skill sets...

Please Rate Yourself:

1=Managing Down 2=Managing Across 3=Managing Up

Circle strongest skill set: 1   2   3

Circle the greatest area of
development skill set: 1   2   3

What's the "one thing" you will do in each of these skill sets to grow closer to elite over the next 120 Days?

Skill Set 1 _____

_____

_____

Skill Set 2 _____

_____

_____

Skill Set 3 _____

_____

_____

EXERCISE

"I have worked with Coach for almost twelve years now. Among the many items Coach and I discuss during our regular meetings, I believe the two most important are: how to continually remain focused on the most important initiatives at the moment, and also how to find clarity of purpose at work and home (which isn't easy during these crazy times). He is my mentor, confidant, voice of reason, trail guide (in the business sense), and a true friend. I am grateful to have Coach in my life and in my corner each and every day."

Andy McFetridge, CPWA® CEPA® CRPC®, Head of Strategic Relationships & Investment Specialists

"Coach Brett is an authentic leader who is able to bring out the best in others. He is inquisitive, focused and a forward thinker. He is intentional and genuine in his interactions and creates opportunities for those that he coaches and partners with to dig into their potential."

Juline McMullen, Director of Learning and Development

"If you are looking for a talented coach that truly cares about you and your success, then Coach D is for you. His passion, unique skill set and results-oriented coaching style, motivated me to step outside my comfort zone and unlock my full potential. I'm now "majoring in the majors" as a direct result of his careful guidance and motivation."

James Scally, CFP®, Managing Partner
Heritage Financial

"Coach D is a generational talented coach who has mastered the art of motivation, goal setting, relationship building and teaming. I've had the pleasure of having Coach D as my hockey coach and during that time, he taught me the importance of setting goals and tracking progress; a results focused process that has positively impacted my life and career. #ExpectToWIN"

Kevin Francischelli, Associate, Portfolio Management Reporting & Analysis—Finance at Point72

"Coach Brett has been critical in my development as a manager of people and in keeping my own personal life objectives top of mind. Prior to us working together, I shared with him the lack of intentional efforts put into my people leading skills. All that changed, the day our relationship began. Since we've been working together Coach has given me a skillset that I call on daily, kept me laser focused on what really matters in business and personally, and helped to propel me to places I never thought I could go. To echo words from the cult classic movie Spinal Tap, "This one goes to eleven!" I can't more strongly recommend Coach Brett."

Kent Lepard, RPA, CRPS, Divisional Vice President

"Brett communicates with clarity, intelligence, and enormous energy. His personal coaching activity reveals a sincere passion for helping others reach their goals. Brett is a game-changer!"

Mike Sayles, Managing Partner at StoneTower Search

"So the saying goes, "You are either running your business or it's running you". It is so easy to get caught up in the minutia of business and life and get off track from spending the effort to focus on the right activities that make a successful business. Through your coaching and guidance over the past 13+ years, we have truly learned the importance of goal setting, monitoring progress of stated goals, and accountability. To some, this may sound like Basics 101 but I would argue most professionals don't honestly implement these, and most importantly, follow through on them consistently with clarity and precision like we have with you. Your guidance and coaching is simply the heartbeat of our business now. I am thankful for your professionalism as a coach and grateful for our relationship as friends. You have certainly made a significant difference in the direction of our firm. Thank you for doing what you do and how you do it."

Michael "Mick" Edwards, CIMA®, CRPC®, Managing Director, Partner & Wealth Advisor at Carson Wealth

"It's been a great honor and opportunity for me to work with Coach. His ability to listen, observe, diagnose and coach is Elite. He genuinely cares about what I'm trying to build and where I'm trying to go. At the end of the day, He flat out helps me W.I.N.!"

Nick Hammer, CIMA® CEPA®, Senior Vice President, Divisional Sales Manager

Tip #41
Know You're Only One YES Away

If you never ask, the answer will always be NO.

We are the passionate sort. We chase our dreams; we put in the work and the time to earn everything we're yearning for. We're not afraid of blood, sweat, tears...and there's nothing we won't do in order to reach our goals.

And yet, there's the issue of asking for what we want.

It's as if asking is a sign of weakness, or a signal that we're not willing to create it, or go get it for ourselves.

Nothing could be further from the truth. What great leaders across space and time have discovered is when they find the courage to ask for what they want, they are always only one YES away from getting it. They have learned that when they don't ask, it's worse than getting a NO—because they will always wonder about what could have been. They'll always question their choice, their competency to lead people when they, themselves, have struggled with being vulnerable enough to simply open their mouths and ask.

What have you been wanting and needing—but have refused yourself the privilege of asking for?

What if you got a YES to the one thing you want more than anything else?

And how will you know how that feels if you never ask?

Asking for the YES

Many of us envy those people who ask for what they want without hesitation. And what might separate you from them is the fact that they often got what they wanted as a child—so they have little fear of rejection. Maybe your parents raised a reasonable, respectful man or woman by telling you NO. And now here you are, a nice guy or gal who questions your right to ask for what you want.

Maybe you're not considering the times you asked for what you deserved, for what was best for you...and got the YES.

It's a double-edged sword, but that doesn't mean you can't turn that sword around and use it to your advantage.

Here are a few pieces of advice for learning to *ask*:

- **Be Reasonable:** You're not going to walk into your first day as a team leader and ask for the CEO position. You might, however, put in two solid years of trans-formative service and then ask for a promotion. Understand there are steps involved, and that the YES you're looking for should be within reason.

- **Aim High:** Just because you're being reasonable doesn't mean you have to settle. Do not downgrade your dreams or ask for anything less than you can handle or that you know you deserve. In fact, ask for just a bit more than you think might be appropriate at this moment and watch what happens.

- **Identify your Fear:** Remember that **F.E.A.R.** stands for **F**alse **E**vidence **A**ppearing **R**eal, meaning that whatever is holding you back is probably just a limiting belief, or a perception that is sabotaging your chances of success. Examine your past, your present situation…and name the thing you're afraid of. Call it out, let it know you've blown its cover, and move forward in spite of it.

- **Keep it Simple:** Sometimes, we think we have one chance to ask for what we want, and so we pile together lots of requests and lots of reasons why we should have those things. This not only makes you appear unsure of what you want, it flusters the person you're asking. Ask for one thing. Have one really good reason. And they'll have more reason to say YES.

- **Bring Value:** People rarely say YES just to make you happy; there's got to be a benefit in it for them, too. So no matter what you're asking for—a sale, a promotion, a favor—make sure you're bringing value to the table.

What's the difference between asking and getting a NO, and never asking at all?

When you get a NO, you might also get feedback about how you can get a YES in the future; you can have pride because you tried, and the next time won't be so difficult.

When you never ask, you'll simply never know.

Go ahead and ask. And always remember that you're only one YES away from getting exactly what you want.

> *"Make excuses or Make it HAPPEN, YES You Can!"*
> *—Coach Davenport*

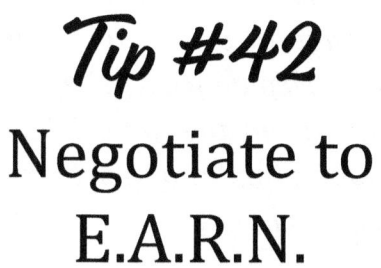

Tip #42
Negotiate to E.A.R.N.

Behind every earned win is a foolproof strategy.

What separates master negotiators (the ones who get what they want) from the rest? How do they seem to win at every turn? How do they come out of every meeting with the upper hand? And EARN the respect of their clients and peers?

Expert negotiation is not for the faint of heart. It requires tremendous confidence and a desire to win.

It requires the heart of a lion—one that is prepared, rehearsed, agile, responsive...and unwilling to settle for anything less than achievement of the goal.

The Best Strategy Wins

Maddie is waiting in the Washington Room for her client's entourage to arrive. Her flight landed two hours ago (as she'd planned it), she's already grabbed a cup of coffee from the hotel lobby, and she has placed full-color samples of her marketing strategy on the table, at each seat.

She's expecting eight people. She knows their names and positions. She knows how long they've worked with the company, as well as each one's professional experience and business philosophy.

Her presentation will appeal to Shapiro's penchant for risk-taking, and she has responses prepared for when Smith starts worrying about cost and when Jones comes back with his need for "traditional" materials. She will ask for 850K, but will not settle for less than her baseline of 750K.

Maddie can barely contain her excitement. She's prepared, she's energized, she's confident. She will win this.

Across the six-lane highway, at the Hyatt, Angela is trying to figure out how to fit herself and all her bags through the revolving door. She didn't have time to gather the materials she would need for today's pitch, so she brought everything from the office.

Would she have enough copies? Would they notice she cut corners to get it produced in time?

What was the name of the CEO again?

She stumbles to the front desk. "The Lincoln Room?"

The clerk points in the direction of the meeting room.

As Angela heaves the bags over her shoulder, she wonders not only if they'll like the campaign, but what price they'll offer.

Negotiations carry a common overtone, and it has to do with "winging it." After all, a discussion is expected. There are a number of variables that can, and will, arise. And no one can predict, with 100% certainty, how any given negotiation will turn out.

That's why you need an unshakable plan. Because there's potential for so many variables during negotiations, you must counter-balance that with the foolproof E.A.R.N. Strategy:

1. **Expect to Win:** If you leave any negotiation to fate, it will not go your way, or you will get less than you deserve. Go in knowing you will win, with confidence. Have faith that what you have to offer is what they need the most. Envision victory. Manifest your triumph.

2. **Analyze:** Prepare responses for every possible scenario, so you can feel confident no matter what happens. This means knowing as much as possible about the company, the people, the circumstance…you've got to do your homework.

3. **Relate:** When you listen, you're not simply letting them know you care about their needs. You're gathering information so you can win. Focus on the words they use and the cues they provide—then respond in one of the ways you've prepared.

4. **Negotiate:** The art of negotiation does require compromise; however, that doesn't mean you have to settle for less than you wanted. It simply means you've got to ask for more than you want. Then, you get what you want *and* they feel like they've won, too.

"Run to the roar with confidence…"

—Coach Davenport

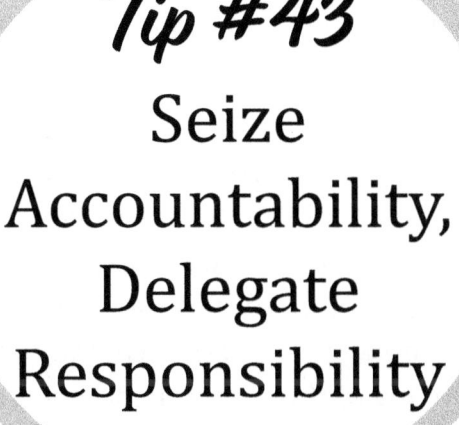

Tip #43
Seize Accountability, Delegate Responsibility

When everyone is responsible, the result can be that no one is accountable.

Have you ever been in a situation where the boss says, "It's everybody's job to get this done"?

In rare cases, everyone will work together to achieve that one mission.

More often, one person will take charge and command the troops.

Most often, the task never gets completed; everyone is expecting the "other person" to do the work.

This type of scenario usually doesn't end well because everyone is Responsible…but no one is Accountable.

What's the difference?

Responsibility means you're charged with a task. Accountability means you have ownership of the outcome. For instance, if you're Responsible for making sure everyone is notified of a meeting tomorrow at 2 pm, it's your job to get all of them in the right spot at the right time. If any of those people do not show up, or go to the wrong site, you are Accountable.

In many ways, you're not Accountable until something goes wrong. It can seem unfair—particularly if you didn't recognize you would be Accountable from the start.

And for this reason, it's a great idea to Seize Accountability before anything has a chance to go awry. Knowing the effects and consequences ahead of time will not only inspire you to track the progress of any given project, it will boost the entire team's chances of success.

The Power of Accountability

On an NFL team, every player has one principal task. Call the play, hike the ball, pass the ball, catch the ball, run the ball, defend the ball or make the interception or the tackle. When any player doesn't do his job, he's reprimanded, benched or traded…and all that is overseen by the head coach because he's Accountable for the team's record.

When the team's owner approaches that head coach with questions about why the team isn't winning, that head coach can't blame the offensive coaching staff, or the defensive line; he alone is Accountable for making sure everything is running smoothly and reflected in the team's record.

Whatever went wrong went wrong because he allowed it to happen.

When you are Accountable for an outcome, you will do whatever it takes to make sure that outcome benefits everyone involved. And by "do whatever it takes," I do not mean that you put the burden of every task onto your own shoulders.

By delegating tasks, and narrowing one broad Responsibility into smaller, more manageable ones, you are essentially making people Accountable for their own part of the project, which naturally makes everyone answerable for their roles...and therefore more likely to get the job done, well.

You might also "do whatever it takes" by tracking the progress of a project, detecting potential problems, and remedying them before they balloon into something that cannot be fixed. This pre-emptive way of thinking is indicative of someone who knows they're Accountable.

But why would anyone deliberately choose Accountability?

Leaders are naturally drawn to it. They do not shy away from challenges, the potential for failure, or an obligation to lead their teams to victory. In many ways, simply being Responsible for something isn't enough for driven leaders. They want more—and that "more" is a unique brand of ownership called *Accountability*.

> *"The 'BEST' ability is ACCOUNT-ABILITY!"*
> —Coach Davenport

Tip #44
Prescribe Your Own P.I.P.

Be proactive in You: the one area where you have complete control.

A Performance Improvement Program, or P.I.P., could be called the *Thin Ice* of the workforce. If you receive one of these written documents from your boss, it means your performance has been less than expected; it means you've disappointed those who are counting on you. To be blunt, you're on the path to being fired, and this is your last chance to turn that around.

These *Thin Ice* documents don't materialize from *Thin Air*. In fact, ask anyone who's ever received one and they'll tell you that it came as no surprise. They might even tell you that when they were called into the boss' office, they had expected to be canned, but were happy to see they were not only getting another chance, but had a concrete strategy for improvement.

Since that's the case, I have a question: If you can see that P.I.P. coming, why not preempt it by prescribing your very own Performance Improvement Program? Before the boss has to do it for you? This will not only save your reputation in the workplace, it will advance you along the leadership path and put valuable self-auditing skills into practice.

Chances are you know what's keeping you from being employee of the month—but you don't have the resources or the discipline to fix it.

That's about to change.

Customize Your Own P.I.P. and Call it *Goal Setting*

When things aren't going as well as anticipated, it's your job, as a leader, to take matters into your own hands and intercept the trouble that's coming down the road.

Being proactive may keep you off thin ice and on solid ground, but more importantly, it will prove your ability to be an autonomous, accountable leader. It will prove you have what it takes to self-assess, self-correct and WIN.

Using a standard P.I.P. format, here are the steps for setting goals and improving your performance:

1. **Name the area in need of improvement.** Maybe you're getting critical feedback in this area. Or, maybe you're struggling to deliver what you would consider "quality" work. Name the problem; that's always the first step to finding a solution.

2. **Describe expectations.** If you were performing at top-level in this area, what would that look like? Envision high achievement and express it.

3. **Name helpful resources.** You may not have the tools you need to succeed in this area. Whom can you consult with? Where can you go to learn? What help is available to those struggling in this area?

4. **Find someone who will hold you accountable.** When the bar is raised, you've got to ask someone to make sure you're reaching, or exceeding, the level of that bar. Without accountability, it's too easy to cut corners and slip back into old, damaging habits.

5. **Establish consequences.** If your employer was the one prescribing this improvement strategy, there would be consequences if you didn't make corrections. Work with your accountability partner to determine what will happen if you don't do the work.

6. **Track your progress.** In order to make progress, you've got to measure what matters. Provide yourself with proof that

you're moving forward, as well as evidence that your plan may not be working. Keep an open mind and adjust as needed.

Let's face it: we all know when we're under-performing. There's a lack of response from others, a lack of pride in ourselves and a lack of goal-oriented results. This is true in a marriage, as a parent, in social groups, on a team and in the workplace.

So let's get proactive about leadership performance. Let's be honest with ourselves about the areas in which we're lacking and fortify them now—before someone else does.

"If we don't take care of ourselves, we won't be able to take care of others."

—Coach Davenport

#1 TEAM!

Coach Davenport's Exercise for You and/or Your Team!

Self Assessment Examination:

Rating

1 = Major area of opportunity

2-6 = Displays range of development

7 = Major area of strength

* After each area of "honest" assessment. Please write down the #1 activity you will commit to in order to achieve your 52 week goal!

"Study the past. Live the moment. Plan the future."®

—Coach Davenport

Prescribe Your Own P.I.P. | 235

	52 Weeks Ago	Today	Expectations 52 Weeks from Today

Mentally Fit _____   _____   _____

#1 Activity

Physically Fit _____   _____   _____

#1 Activity

Financially Fit _____   _____   _____

#1 Activity

Spiritually Fit _____   _____   _____

#1 Activity

Family Fit _____   _____   _____

#1 Activity

Leadership Fit _____   _____   _____

#1 Activity

Your Wildcard _____   _____   _____

#1 Activity

EXERCISE

"Coach Davenport is the kind of person who makes you want to be the best version of yourself! His guidance has made a huge difference in how I run my business and now guide my employees. He gives you goals that are attainable and makes you realize that anything is achievable through hard work and dedication! I am forever grateful to have his knowledge and will continue to learn through him! I could honestly write a book on how your inspiring words and problems solving skills have helped me!"

Kim Chamberlain, Owner at Adonia Salon & Spa

"Brett Davenport lives and demonstrates by his example, the commitment to learning, growth and development that he coaches and leads others to embrace. I join the chorus of recommendations that highlight Brett's inspirational energy, focus and drive. Brett's communication and interpersonal skills are a cut above —he is one of those rare and wonderful people who is completely present during a conversation. He takes time to listen, to care, to relate. It is a joy to know Brett. He walks his talk."

Dr. Julie A. Gedro, Dean of the School of Business at SUNY Empire

"Brett, "Coach", is great at getting people to focus on what is important professionally and personally and them providing the tools to succeed at both."

Michele Butt, AVP, Head of Advisory Analysis, Global Public Markets

"Brett is a pleasure to work with. He sees the angles and presents an objective point of view backed by years of experience. He is a master at top of mind awareness, facilitating mutually agreed upon professional and personal goals. Part of his raw talent is then compelling one to hold themselves accountable for said goals. Fantastic professional coach that I fully endorse."

Chip Saltz, National Sales Manager at Starwood Capital Group: SREIT

"I've worked with Brett Davenport for the last 6 years and highly recommend him for any business leader looking to take their management and leadership to the next level. He cares deeply about everyone he works with and does a great job focusing only on what matters."

Sammy Azzouz, JD, CFP®, President and CEO of Heritage Financial Services, LLC

"I would highly recommend Brett in any aspect of the business field, he is a strong leader and a positive motivator."

Kim Gage, Former Sr. Licensed Loan Officer/Branch Manager

"Whatever challenges, opportunities, or successes you have in life or business, Brett has the ability to overcome, guide and celebrate with you. I have witnessed firsthand, Brett's passion is helping you make your life better than it currently is!"

Joseph Arsenault, CFP®, ChFC®, Wealth Manager
Heritage Financial

"I have worked closely with Coach Davenport for 10 years and without embellishment, he has changed my life. Not only has he helped me to excel and perform better with respect to my job, but he has also helped me become a better Husband and Dad. Coach, is all in, and he holds you accountable to changing your behavior, so that you can implement solutions. Finally, he creates a partnership and helps you make changes every step of the way. Undoubtedly, I would not have achieved many of my goals without the guidance, tips and support from Coach. He is the real deal and a phenomenal person, mentor and coach."

Sean Farley, MBA, CEPA®, CRPC®, GFS,
Senior Vice President

"Charismatic, Bright, Articulate, Goal Oriented - just a few of the qualities that come to mind when thinking of Brett. Brett will light up your room with personality and quickly impresses with his leadership and knowledge."

Gary Heenan, Head Hockey Coach
Utica University

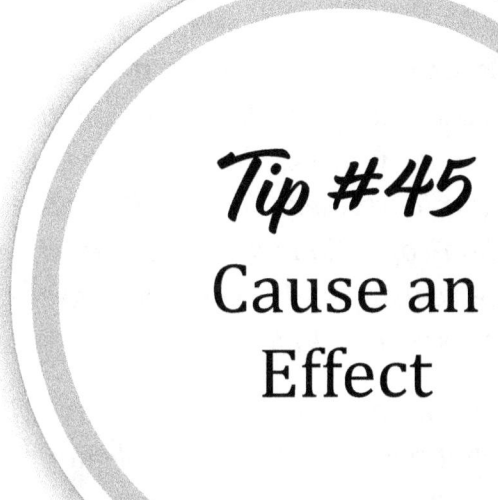

Tip #45
Cause an Effect

Followers are affected; leaders cause effects.

All businesses, organizations and teams with a competitive advantage have at least one thing in common, and that's a proactive strategy.

A leader enacts change, rather than changing after being backed into a corner by forces outside his control.

A leader is a change agent who looks to the landscape ahead and adjusts her strategy according to what she sees.

A leader isn't afraid to be the first person to do something; his only fear is being the last.

A Leader is Proactive, Rather than Reactive

Randy operates a small family diner along Route 88. He's proud of the cozy atmosphere and the steady stream of regular customers. The waitresses take orders on carbon-copy tablets, count out change from an antique register and accept only cash (and the occasional trusted check) for payment.

The diner has been serving the same dishes since 1983. "That's what people like, and people don't like change," says Randy.

And as the area surrounding the diner becomes more built-up with residential neighborhoods, Randy sees an increase in teenagers and families patronizing the restaurant. He also sees a decline in the number of repeat customers. His older clientele is dying. And the numbers prove he's having trouble keeping the interest of a younger crowd.

Ten miles away, also on Route 88, the owner of Tom's Diner took notice to the upswing in new housing development five years ago, and he questioned how well his current business strategy would accommodate that. He noted that not only were young families moving into the area, they were traveling to the city for work.

He studied the practices and popular menu items in the city. What was important to those customers? He learned they were interested in vegan and allergen-

free items, a revolving menu, speed of service and ease of payment.

And so, Tom secured cross-contamination food safety training for his kitchen staff, obtained a food allergen certification, and installed technology that would speed along the ordering and payment processes.

Over the next year, Tom's Diner experienced a spike in profit, mostly due to repeat business from a younger, more progressive customer base.

Randy did his best to keep up. He updated a few of his under-performing menu items, installed a point-of-sale system...but he was too late. The precedent that Tom had set was simply too much to keep up with, retroactively.

If you choose to operate as a reactive leader, you'll be lucky if you're simply left behind. In most cases, the outcome is far worse. You might miss the opportunity of a lifetime because you were too preoccupied with "business as usual." You might allow operations to suffer to the point that important people notice, resulting in irreparable damage to your reputation. Or, you might put yourself and your organization in a frightening financial situation—without enough money in the budget to catch up to where you should have been long ago.

If, however, you take a proactive leadership stance, choosing to look down the road and beat looming challenges with an upfront, positive strategy, you will establish yourself as a fearless change-maker. You will never settle for feeling like a victim. You will enjoy a massive competitive advantage, simply because you're so far ahead. And because you're solving small problems before they have a chance to balloon into something unmanageable, you're operating in a cost-effective manner.

You were not born proactive or reactive. You were not born able or unable to cause an effect.

In every situation, it's a matter of choice.

What will you choose? Will you enact the change that others will respond to? Or will you be the one responding?

Will you be a leader?

Or will you be a follower?

"We have things happen to us; that's called life. We make things happen for us; that's called LIVING."

—Coach Davenport

Tip #46
Keep it Clean

Don't swear; there's always a better word.

When you hear a person using vulgar language on a regular basis, what does it tell you about that person?

That they're a rebel, unbound by the rules of society?

That they have little respect for the institutions and people with which they work?

Or that they lack the vocabulary to fully express themselves?

There seems to have been a recent shift in the acceptance of cursing—but one thing is for sure: No matter what that type of language tells us about the person who's swearing, it's never compatible with leadership.

Curse Words Say More When They're NOT There

When you are in your leadership role, the language you use matters. I would even go so far as to say that in your personal life and social circles, it matters too.

Because once you're a leader in one area of your life, that will (and should) spill over into the rest.

When you refrain from swearing in the presence of your team, customers, investors, colleagues...here's what that says about you:

- You not only have **respect** for your leadership position and the weight it carries, you have respect for the people around you who may not appreciate that type of language.

- You have an **intelligent person's vocabulary**. In other words, you are educated enough to be able to find words to express how you're feeling.

- You inspire **trust**. Your team members know that when you're representing them, you always present yourself (and them, by default) in a professional manner.

- You have **excellent communication skills**. You don't need to rely on expletives to get your point across.

- You exercise **self-control**, meaning you know when particular behaviors are not appropriate.

- You understand the importance of **leading by example**, because you wouldn't want your team representing your organization like a foul-mouthed gang of renegades.

If you have come from another circumstance where cursing is commonplace, or "it's just how you are," it's important to understand that your success as a leader rests on your ability to adjust to your current situation and to lead by example.

By regulating your language, you are demonstrating your ability to manipulate your pre-frontal cortex, or your "thinking brain," where conscious decisions are made. After all, swearing originates in the ancient, or the reptilian, brain. Is that how you want others to view your capacity for leadership?

There are some leaders who might say cursing should be encouraged in social situations with their team, because it fosters bonding, or comradery. I do understand how this might be adopted by some organizations; however, I would ask you to consider what this requires of your team. You'd be asking them not only to use bad language in order to fit in, you'd be asking every one of them to adopt a split culture, in which each has to master two languages, one for the team and one for the public. A company culture is always more effective when it runs through-and-through, in all operations.

When you curse on a regular basis, it loses its impact. If you are angry, or surprised, who will know? How will that be any different than any other day?

I urge you to be more conscious of the language you use, what it says about you, and what it says to your team about themselves.

"Exiting an organization like a professional pays big time dividends sometime in the future."

—Coach Davenport

Tip #47
Take the Most Important Step

The first step is the one that all other steps follow.

Every achievement has one thing in common: it had a first step. The number of steps involved with the attainment of goals varies widely. Some have two steps. Others have hundreds of steps. But what they all share is the start—that very first step.

When a ball is sitting still, it will remain in that state until energy is transferred to it. It must be kicked, or thrown, or pushed...and only then does it have the momentum to move. It will remain in motion until its momentum is transferred to another object.

In this illustration, it's easy to see that procrastination, or fear, most profoundly affects that first step. It's much simpler to *keep* that ball rolling than to *start* it rolling.

The achievement of your goals is no different. Get the ball moving—take that first step—and know that you've completed the most important part.

Your Comfort Zone is Killing your Dreams

Your comfort zone feels so good. It's filled with things you know. It's conventional, predictable…safe.

So is a rut.

When you're in that rut, or that comfort zone, you might acknowledge that you want more, or that you dislike your current situation; however, you also recognize that it's much easier to stick with what you know.

You've heard about the "easy way out." In most cases, it's more like the "easy way in." Staying in that comfort zone, withIN the boundaries you've established for yourself, is the easy way. But it's never the right way.

If you dig yourself out of that rut, you'll have to navigate the rest of the path, which is unknown to you. If you step outside that comfort zone, you might achieve great things, but you'll also feel exposed or vulnerable.

And so, many potential leaders stay in that comfort zone. It's not great, but it's what they know.

What keeps prospective leaders and their goals inside that circle of comfort? It can be attributed to a number of things, but most commonly, there is...

- fear of failure
- heightened expectations
- greater responsibility
- possibility of rejection
- inevitable mistakes
- awkward exposure
- perceptions of incompetency

And so, too many prospective leaders stay holed up in that "comfortable" area, waiting for a perfect, easy, safe opportunity to materialize—an opportunity that feels like it only requires things they already know, things they've already done and nothing they fear.

No opportunity looks like that.

Reaching your goals is going to come with a series of steps that might make you feel exposed, or incompetent at times. These circumstances are all necessary for growth and learning. You simply cannot advance using only what you know right now. You might have the knowledge, but need more people. You might know the people, but need more education. Or, you might have all of that and need skills to bring it all together.

In general, the thing you're missing, or the thing you're most fearful of, is the thing that will move you forward.

It's time to take that first step. Acknowledge your fear and discomfort, and move toward it.

And after you take that first step (which might come in the form of a phone call, an email, a meeting, or an enrollment), notice the exhilaration that comes from that risk. Feel the freedom of operating without confinement and see how many more options are obvious now that you've broken away from the depth of that rut.

The first step will be the most difficult. Prove to yourself you have what is required for taking that first step, and then feel your momentum and your power build as you move through the rest, on your way to achieving that goal and ultimately many more!

> *"The snowball effect is rolling in your favor, keep pressing forward."*
>
> *—Coach Davenport*

Tip #48
Finish It

If you wish to compete, you've got to complete.

Are you someone worth betting on? How can you be sure?

There's one foolproof way to know if you're worth the risk, and that's to ask yourself if you have a finishing record. Do you start projects and not complete them? If so, then no one is going to bet on you. They will not make the investment.

Or, is it important to you that you finish what you start, with the best possible outcome, even if everything didn't go as anticipated? If that's your answer, then the wagers are more likely to start rolling in. That's the reputation you want to have in order to obtain the support you'll need.

Finishing not only accomplishes goals, it builds your good reputation in your company, market, industry or league.

Finishing on a regular basis marks you as a "sure thing," a good investment, a risk worth taking, someone worth following...a leader.

Many Start, but Few Finish

Jared is on a roll. He's scheduled a farm tour of the largest artichoke producer on the west coast, and while he's there, he's hoping to land a deal for the upcoming harvest. He has spoken to three southern California retailers, and they're anxiously awaiting numbers. He has begun to develop a wholesale strategy he will present to the board on Monday.

"Sounds great," says Jill, who has taken Jared out to lunch to discuss the plan for the coming month. "Very ambitious...and it's only the fifth."

"I like to get lots of projects started," replies Jared. "It's how I operate."

As Jill drains her coffee cup and watches Jared's phone light up with incoming messages, she can't help but think of all the emails she's sent to Jared...emails that Jared has never responded to.

Across the restaurant, Michael is meeting with his sales manager. "I'm headed to ABC Artichoke Farms tomorrow morning. I'll be there for most of the week. We've built a good rapport over the last month, and I feel confident I can strike a deal and come back with lots of options for our distributors."

His boss, McKenzie, nods.

"Once I have that in place, I have a number of retailers I will speak with to find the best contract."

"Excellent," replies McKenzie. "Considering your track record for getting things done, and the plan you've got for carrying this one to completion, I think we'll talk about making you team leader when you return."

Jared had become so accustomed to the thrill of starting that he had forgotten about his obligation to finish. His boss is fully aware of his reputation for this behavior, and so Jared will never be elevated to a leadership role until that **A**rea **O**f **D**evelopment, AKA **A.O.D.** becomes a strength...at a minimum.

Michael, on the other hand, has built a reputation for himself that is so foolproof, his boss is talking promotion before he even seals the next deal. That's because his reputation has proven he is highly likely to follow through.

When it comes to finishing what you start, your reputation precedes you.

If, as a leader, you wish to be respected and trusted, you must keep your promises (both spoken and implied) by always finishing what you start. Even if things don't go quite as planned, follow through with integrity.

Do what you say you're going to do, or quit before you finish. Either way, everyone will notice.

"We execute goals, our competition brags about their aspiration's AKA resolutions."

—Coach Davenport

Coach Davenport's Exercise for You and/or Your Team!

Let's set your goals today...

3 Personal

Goal	Picture	Date to Celebrate Goal Attainment
_____	☐	_____
_____	☐	_____
_____	☐	_____

3 Professional

Goal	Picture	Date to Celebrate Goal Attainment
_____	☐	_____
_____	☐	_____
_____	☐	_____

"Brett has many good qualities. What I enjoy most about Brett is, he's a cool cat, he's calm, he listens and he does not become flustered >>> even in the crazy times. You can depend on Brett for solid advise in all situations. His irenic manner always comes through—he's an enjoyable person to be around, and an outstanding Coach."

Sue Pregartner, Principal, Founder at Intrinzik Creative Consulting

"Met Brett as he was partnering with colleagues to build a new success model in Utica, New York. His vision, leadership, and coaching skills gave new life to his agency by energizing his team. As head of community affairs at the time, I was happy that his model also embraced outreach to his neighbors in need, which, in turn, helped strengthen his new business model."

Mary O'Malley, Fully retired at GoodDoers and Scribes

"Brett Davenport has made a tremendous impact on the growth and success of our firm. His steady guidance, knowledge of the industry and consistent follow through have kept us on task, making sure that my partner and I keep the "main things the MAIN THING!" Further to that, his care for us and our families has been a tremendous blessing to each of us individually, and as a firm collectively."

Karl V. Kimball, CLU®, ChFC®, Managing Director, Partner & Wealth Advisor at Carson Wealth

"I have had the privilege to know Mr. Davenport (Coach D) for over 10 years. He has been a mentor to myself and others growing up since I can remember. As recently jumping into my career in Sales I have reached out to Coach D for advice and leadership. He has given me advice and played a role in my success that he may not realize. Coach D brings energy to a room that I wish all leaders and managers could replicate. He has a constant positive attitude and will do whatever it takes to help you succeed and drive that winning mindset into you. Anyone who wants to better themselves both personally or professionally should consult with Coach D. Thanks for everything!"

Mike Vanderhoof Jr., Territory Sales Manager, Ultrasound at Siemens Healthineers

"Brett has been instrumental in my growth; he has pushed me to be the best version of myself in career and spirit. His wholistic approach to achieve career and personal goals fosters a balance between the motivation to succeed at work but never at the expense of what is meaningful at home."

Melissa Mattison, Chief Operating Officer, Heritage Financial

"Brett is an incredibly insightful leader in our industry. He has a no-nonsense mind who understands the profession, its challenges and unbridled opportunities. This is an impressive individual who is as candid as he is imaginative."

Dr. Larry Barton, Threat and Risk Consultant

"My team and I have worked closely with Coach D for 7 years now and we've had excellent results! He brings the best out of me and my team by helping us think outside the box, make major business decisions, strategize for the future, formulate personal and business goals, and makes us accountable to get the job done. Coach D constantly raises the bar and has helped us accomplish more than we could have ever imagined. I highly recommend Coach Brett Davenport if you want to take your level of productivity and business to the next level!"

Chuck Bean, Founder and Chairman at Heritage Financial Services, LLC

"Brett and I began working together in March of 2020. Since then, we were all hit with Covid 19, the world shut down and my work and personal life routine was abruptly disrupted. Coach kept me focused on my goals and provided explicit tools to adapt quickly and smoothly to a new way of thinking and creative ways to expect to win! A year we will all certainly remember, I am so grateful to be working with Coach. 2020 was one of the most successful years of my career and a springboard to great things to come. As we start year number 4 together, all I can say is thank you, Coach!"

Leo Reed, Managing Director, Nuveen Taft-Hartley Institutional Development Managing

Tip #49
Treat all Days Equally

Give every day an equal opportunity to be amazing.

Monday is a drag. Tuesday is the most productive day of the week. Wednesday is hump day, and your last chance to set goals for Friday. On Thursday, you try to get everything done, to ease tomorrow's pressure. Friday is for wrapping up loose ends and preparing for the weekend. Saturday is for play. Sunday is for rest. And Sunday night is for getting ready to do it all over again.

If you subscribe to this weekly formula (or anything similar to it), then the only day that should be bringing anything big—in terms of opportunities, advancements and wins—is Tuesday. Wednesday and Thursday are close runners-up, but they're on the downhill side of the week, making them less likely to hold professional promise.

I'll say it: This is nuts.

And yet, so many of us take part in this limiting way of thinking about our work weeks.

There's a better way—a way that will result in far more opportunities than you've been imagining are possible.

Opportunity does not Know what Day it is

Have you ever written off an entire day just because you have a dentist appointment in the afternoon? Or because you have to meet with your child's principal after school? It's not uncommon, and you're not alone.

Many of us tend to expect opportunity when it's convenient for us. But here's the cold, hard truth: Opportunity is not Opportune. It doesn't wait until you're sitting at your desk, or for when you have a whole day to do nothing other than chase it.

Instead, it's going to come your way when circumstances are ideal for the person offering the opportunity, when all the ingredients for that opportunity have been added, or when, simply stated, it's supposed to happen.

As a leader, you're in charge. You're organized, you have control over your environment and you have a strategy.

That does not mean, however, that you can control when opportunities will surface.

Often, the best opportunities will show up at the most inopportune times...or at least it can seem that way because opportunity is not concerned with your personal or professional timeline. It happens when it happens, whether you feel like you're ready or not.

It's time to stop reserving Tuesday for big things. It's also time to stop ignoring opportunities that wink at you in the fog of Monday mornings and in the flurry of Friday afternoons.

Instead, open every day with the intention of finding the opportunity it holds. Don't ask if there will be a prospect for advancement today, know that it's there and set out to find it, regardless of the day of the week.

Trust that the opportunity is there, and take responsibility for uncovering it. Know that no matter what the nature of that opportunity may be, it has arrived at precisely the right time, and it's up to you to seize it with all your heart.

> *"The best thing about today is that we have an opportunity to make it count."*
>
> *—Coach Davenport*

Make Your Best *BETTER!*

#1

Tip #50
Go from Worst to First

The one in last place is the one to watch.

Who doesn't love an underdog story? Who doesn't love to watch the *Bad News Bears* climb the bracket and win the championship?

Most of us enjoy seeing the dark horse take the lead... from the stands. But when it comes to being that underdog, or that dark horse, it can be easy to feel discouraged, or to lose faith in our own ability to overcome gigantic odds.

However, there is a method you can use—in any circumstance—to climb the ladder of success and take you (and your team) from worst to first.

A Best-Practice Team-Building Exercise

The St. Louis Blues were ranked dead last in their 31-team NHL league in early January 2019. The team had never even won a finals game. And yet, five months later, they clinched the title. They won the Stanley Cup.

How did they do it? How did The Blues fire through the competition, all the way to league dominance, for the first time ever in 52 years?

I'm just guessing, but maybe someone told them they couldn't do it. That's one way to light a fire under a future leader.

Another possibility is a more reliable method—a team-building exercise that focuses on the positive so that it can expand and fuel your quest for success.

This exercise can be carried out between a supervisor and employee, a coach and his team, a manager and her division...during impromptu or scheduled meetings, at any time of the year.

It goes like this:

A. What is the **#1 most SUCCESSFUL activity** from your business plan, performed during the current year?

B. What is the **#1 activity that UNDERPERFORMED** to the greatest degree, and WHY did it not work as successfully as you had expected?

C. What is the **#1 activity from your business plan (maybe a new addition) that you will**

EXECUTE to the best of your ability in the next ___ days in order to WIN this year?

From the asking and answering of these questions will spring astounding dialogue that will reveal a clear path to success. A positive platform for sharing ideas will develop. You will uncover techniques that work for moving your organization forward, and the concept of business planning will take on an entirely new hopeful spin. This exercise will come to be the foundation for growing your organization—one team member, one team, one obstacle at a time.

There's something charming about a team moving from last place to first place. It's the type of story we all want to believe in.

It's time to believe in it—and in yourself. The psychology of the underdog is more powerful than many of us realize. You see, when you're down, you have nothing to lose. You can give it everything you have without fear. The human spirit fights harder when the stakes are higher, and that resolve is what drives us to grow increasingly more competent, capable and victorious.

If you're down, if you're the worst, can you embrace the possibility of being first? It's time to get used to the idea, because the odds are about to shift in your favor.

"Yes, anything is possible in business, sports or YOUR LIFE."
—Coach Davenport

This Will Be Your #1 Challenge/ Exercise from Coach Davenport if You Want to Achieve All Others at an Elite Level!

What is your #1 area of development, AKA A.O.D.? _____

Why did you choose this one? _____
_____

How will you convert this A.O.D. into a strength? _____

When this A.O.D. becomes a strength, what opportunity will it create for you? _____
_____

Who will hold you ACCOUNTABLE? _____

When do you EXPECT you will be ready to conquer your next A.O.D. up?_____

Thank you for participating in your relentless pursuit to…

MAKE YOUR BEST BETTER!

Coach Davenport #1

"As I have worked with "Coach" for over five years now, he has helped launch my management career. Helping me navigate the dangerous waters of middle management and giving me the tools to ensure my team performs at a very high level. All one needs to do is listen and Coach will give you the keys to the castle one at a time.

Having played in the NFL, I know what makes a coach good and what makes one great. The great ones can identify strengths and areas of development very quickly. They build on the strengths and convert the necessary areas of development into strengths, so that the individual can perform at an elite level. I'm lucky to be working with Coach Davenport! He has been instrumental in ensuring my second career will be my last career, he is truly one of the greats!"

Peter Monty, Divisional Vice President, First Eagle Investment Management

"I have been working with Coach Davenport for over 11 years and continue to love our monthly coaching calls. That regular accountability has helped us achieve many personal and professional goals together through the years bringing multiple sales and performance awards. His positivity and attitude of "Expecting to Win" is contagious and has spread through my team in all the right ways. Reading this book and using his approach will help keep focus on that which matter most in your personal and business lives!"

Joe Smith, Divisional Vice President

"Brett Davenport has become my most trusted business advisor and someone I now consider a dear friend. As a coach, he guides with integrity, enthusiasm, knowledge, experience and the highest level of leadership. I can unequivocally say Brett has enriched my personal and professional life in ways I didn't know were possible. In a world full of so-called "gurus" and self-proclaimed "experts", Brett Davenport is the real deal!"

Brent Niblo, Owner of Live Free Advisors

"I was fortunate enough to have "Coach" Brett as my coach, mentor for a number of years. Brett has amazing energy and brings 100% to every meeting. I found Brett to be very insightful and certainly made me see situations in a different light. Even to this day, in certain circumstances that come up, I think to myself what would Coach have said/done... and it usually makes me stop and think through my response a bit longer which has never led me in the wrong direction. Through Brett's guidance, reflections and insightful and candid discussions, I feel like I became a better worker, more effective manager and felt much happier overall."

Effie Duros Georgountzos, Director, Financial Analysis

"Brett is a mentor and sales coach and is outstanding at what he does. Highly recommend him to anyone seeking sales training and coaching. His approach to sales coaching is direct, effective, and repeatable. His passion for sales training and coaching shows from the first day you meet him. Hence, why he is an excellent sales and business coach."

Justin Jordan, Internal Sales Director

"I have had the pleasure to work with Brett my entire life. He is extremely focused on not only helping you excel in both your career and your life but making sure you realize that this version of yourself was there all along. My favorite part about working with Coach Davenport is he knows exactly how to inspire you to be the best version of yourself. I would highly recommend him, "my Dad" to anyone who is looking to improve in any aspect of business or life."

Harrison Davenport, Sr. Business Development Manager at Sotero

"Coach "Dad" Davenport, If you want to WIN both personally & professionally Coach D has all the tools and expertise to get you where you want to be. Coach knows how to get the most out of you by leading by example, he is the only person I know that will go on the journey with you, through the ups and downs and will celebrate when you reach the TOP! My Dad will inspire you to WIN each and everyday!"

Connor Davenport, Account Manager at OraPharma Inc.

"I have known Brett both personally and professionally for over 23 years. I can honestly say that I have learned an incredible amount of life skills and professional skills from him. His energy, ability to coach and guide through his experiences have been a valuable part of my development as a sales professional and individual. Any organization that would utilize his skill set in development and coaching would set themselves on a path for success!"

Mark Kotary, State Farm Insurance Agent/Owner

"I will never forget the day I walked into Brett's office for an interview for my first "real" sales job. Brett's outgoing personality, energy and positive attitude were immediately embracing and enthusiastic. In sharing his vision and his passion for the insurance business and coaching others, I was excited for the opportunity ahead of me. Brett made that dream a reality! Brett's mentorship, strong leadership skills, coaching, enthusiasm and encouragement were instrumental in achieving sales success as an agent and then as a sales manager achieving national recognition with our team, in an industry where what we did every day had a positive impact on other people's lives. Fast forward 25 years later and I now have my own successful sales business helping others to achieve their dreams and goals. I will never forget the foundational skills and motivation that have contributed to both my career and personal successes. Following Brett throughout the years and his own professional achievements, it is clearly apparent that Brett continues to touch the lives of many people through his ongoing positive outlook and passionate energy for helping others."

Sharon Bean, REALTOR®,
Professional Real Estate Consultant at Bean Group

"Brett has been an excellent coach to our executive team. He really takes the time to understand people and the situation before making any recommendations, and he really excels in helping people navigate their professional and personal goals. Brett is one of the most positive people you will ever meet, regardless of the situation!"

Kevin Webb, CFO Norbella Inc.

"One of the toughest realizations any successful leader must inevitably come to is that they really aren't as great a leader as they think. They say behind every great man, there is a great woman. Well, I say that behind every great leader, there is a great mentor. Brett is that mentor.

As the Ground Force Commander of special operations forces during multiple combat deployments, I have depended upon Brett for his expertise, advice, and guidance countless times. As a leadership coach, Brett has trained me to focus on leadership tactics that are effective and catered specifically to my team in order to achieve success in situations where the cost of failure is literally death. Brett has helped to point out the times when I may be self-limiting my own potential and has been there to reassure me and guide me towards metrics of success that I foolishly believed were outside of my reach. Brett has also served as a sounding board and sanity check for my ideas and has helped to prioritize personal goals and develop an aggressive course of action for not only meeting, but also exceeding those goals. He has played the role as an invaluable leadership weapon in my personal armory.

Throughout my career I have had the opportunity to be around many incredible leaders and have seen far too many ineffective leaders. Both of those distinctly different groups of individuals would have benefited greatly from a leadership coaching session with Brett Davenport."

Brian Gleason, Field Associate at Atlas Holdings
Former Navy Seal

"I have been lucky enough to know Brett for about six years. Aside from his genuine kind and thoughtful spirit- I think his best quality is how he always leads by example. While Brett is in incredible coach he is also an impressive individual that gives time and energy to every person that crosses his path. I admire his enthusiasm and ability to make everyone feel important."

Jaime Waldecker, Director of Events at Expect Miracles Foundation—Financial Services Against Cancer

"Brett is an amazing leadership coach who is very professional, I would highly recommend him!"

Adel Wilson, M.A., Media Coach for Entrepreneurs & Professionals

"Working with Brett was truly an enriching experience both professionally and personally. His approach to team management is something I still use today. He applies same approach to personal life for balance. The skills he shared have opened numerous doors and changed many relationships for me in a positive manner. My time with him was worth more than any other trainings or coaching sessions I have had. Great job, Coach!!! Keep it going!"

Peter Rossi, Director, Front Line Risk, Global Markets at Citizens Bank

"Brett has a knack at leading people and teams to great success! He is personable and helps people to achieve projects and accomplish goals that they did not think was possible. If your organization needs someone to help your teams become more effective, Brett can be the mentor and coach to help you get to the next level."

Dr. Amy Valente, Retired Professor of Business

"Brett taught me "Interviewing" skills and techniques. As we worked together I gained confidence and was able to grow my skills through role play and story telling. Brett was a huge reason I was able to get my current job! I highly recommend all the services he offers!"

Madeline Signorelli, Sr. Logistics Incident Analyst at Transaver LLC

"Brett has been my coach for just under 5 years and has completely brought my business to the next level. He's invaluable to myself and my team, in fact I consider him part of my team. I have and would recommend him to anyone looking to be a better leader, coach, and team member."

Seth Renaud, President at C.I.G. Private Wealth Management, LLC

"I have always utilized the services of a professional mentor throughout my 34 year career as a physical therapist and owner of a mid-sized therapy practice. I contacted Brett to assist me in moving from a manager of my practice to prepare it for sale to another entity. Brett's confidence, competence, courage and calm inspired me from our first meeting. He taught me how to hold people accountable, including myself, and taught me how to be a leader instead of a manager. I can recommend his services with the highest degree of confidence. Brett will be an asset to any business or individual that retains his services."

Dana Mandel, Physical Therapist, Founder of Lifespan

"Brett Davenport and I have known each other and worked closely together for the better part of 4 decades. Over the last 13+ years he has been my 'Coach'. During this time I have reached goals and objectives that once seemed unattainable. Coach Davenport is one of the greatest motivators and leader of people that I have had the privilege to work with. If you are looking to take yourself or your team to new levels of success and obtain goals that don't appear reachable then you need Coach Davenport. His proven techniques will help you solidify the goal, set a timeline, prioritize activities and ultimately hold you accountable. He is a proven winner, whether on the golf course, on the gridiron, in a marathon, or in the boardroom. Take your life and your profession to the pinnacle, work with Coach."

Christopher Mee, Managing Director, Distribution at Insperex

This Doesn't Have to be Goodbye

This is your #1 Day! Once you have read and applied all 50 Tips to the advancement of your coaching or leadership role, consider reaching out to me via LinkedIn, email or handwritten note.

I would be honored to become your Personal / Professional / Business / Executive / Performance / Life / Accountability Coach or to be unleashed as your next Motivational / Breakout / Workshop Speaker— to make you and your team's Best even Better!

(888) 5 YES U CAN
info@bmdleadershipinstitute.com
www.coachdavenport.com
BMD Leadership Institute, Inc.
144 Genesee Street
Suite 102-111
Auburn, NY 13021

#Expect2Win
#YesYouCan
#MakeYourBestBetter
#SteadfastLeadership
#TOMA
#LeadershipPlaybook
#CoachingYourWayToSuccess
#America'sTopRatedAccountabilityCoach
#StudythePastLivetheMomentPlantheFuture

Brett M. Davenport

"Leading Authority on Personal Sustainability, Goal Attainment and Leadership" Motivate and Inspire Others!

The Ideal Professional Speaker for Your Next Event!

To Schedule Brett To Speak at Your Event:
Call: 1-888-5-YES U CAN
Visit: www.bmdleadershipinstitute.com
or Email: info@bmdleadershipinstitute.com

MOTIVATE AND INSPIRE OTHERS!
"Share These Books"

To Receive Special Quantity Discounts of Brett's Book(s)

Call: 1-888-5-YES U CAN

Visit: www.bmdleadershipinstitute.com

or Email: info@bmdleadershipinstitute.com

ABOUT BRETT M. DAVENPORT

Brett M. Davenport aka Coach Davenport, started his career in the Financial Services Industry in 1988. During his career he took many underperforming organizations from worst to first and champions from best to better! He built organizations from scratch through hiring what he refers to as #1 Draft Picks, challenged them to embrace change, set balanced goals, be ACCOUNTABLE and created an "Expect to WIN" Mindset! Every team he led ultimately finished 1st!

He has a Master's Degree in Management. In-addition, he is an Annual Judge for Syracuse University's Whitman School of Management.

In 2009 Coach founded BMD Leadership Institute, where he is "America's Top Rated Accountability Coach" for LEADERS in the Financial Services Industry and beyond! He has had over 10,000 One on One Coaching Session and is a 2-time #1 International Best-Selling Author! He travels all over the USA as a Motivational Speaker; inspiring individuals, teams & organizations to "Turn Strategy into Execution... both Personally and Professionally"! Coach is also known for his Game Changing Workshops in the areas of Leadership, Team Building, Goal Setting and Family 1st to name a few!

Coach played Semi-Pro Football, ran the 2012 Boston Marathon (8) Half Marathons (6) 15K's (2) Tough Mudders (1) GoRuck Tough Challenge 2015 (1) GoRuck Constellation Beta 2017 (2) 70 Mile Endurance Canoe Races 1988 & 2018 (1st Leg of the Triple Crown) and (2) Triathlons '18 & '19!

1st Hole-in-One was on June 20th, 2010 (186 yard Par 3, with a 4 iron). What makes this so special, it was on Father's Day at his Father's course with his Father and two Sons as a foursome!

2013–014 Auburn High School Varsity Ice Hockey Team Won their Division, Won the Section 3 Championship, made it to the Frozen 4 NYS Semi-Final Game and finished #3 in New York State... all 1st time accomplishments for Auburn's program! In-addition, during his 5 years as Coach the team made the playoffs each year and qualified for NYSPHSAA's Scholar Athlete Award each of his last 4 years!

Coach D is married to his Beautiful Bride now for 32 years, they have 2 Amazing Sons 30 & 29 years old and most recently a Wonderful Daughter-in-Law!

#1 TEAM!

www.ingramcontent.com/pod-product-compliance
Lightning Source LLC
Chambersburg PA
CBHW050856160426
43194CB00011B/2180